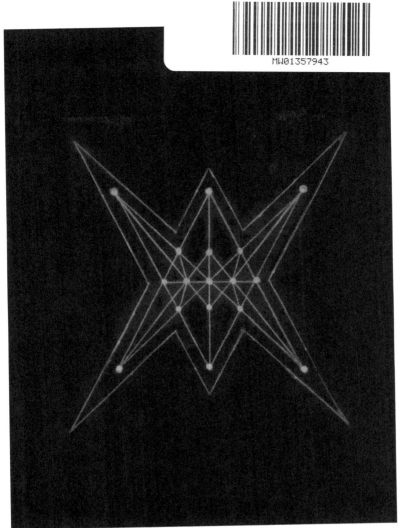

Star of Satanic Creation

The Satanic Bible 2012

by

Rev. Caesar 999

Copyright © 1999 All Rights Reserved
George A. Hart / Rev. Caesar 999

ISBN 13: 978-0-9840313-1-3

Table of Contents

Part I Church Introduction 9
Part II Church Orders 21
Part III Church Principles 31
Part IV Church Regulations 53
Part V Church Goals 83
Part VI Church Rituals and Ceremonies 99
Part VII Church Holy Days 105
Part VIII The Great House of Polygamy 109
Part IX Advanced Church Principles 115
Part X The New Church Sciences 123
Part XI Temple of Kama or Temple of Satanic Kali 129
Part XII Satanic Evolution The Fall of Laveyan Satanism 137
Part XIII The Nine Satanic Statements 175

Part I Church Introduction

Introduction

I am the Rev. Caesar 999 and this is my Satanic Bible. I'd like to now introduce you to my religion under the spiritual name of Vampir Satanism 999 and my first temple as Satan's Divine Vampir Temple which I also call the Church of The Antichrist 999. The time has come for us to examine my beliefs more closely. I'm going to break them down as simply as I can, for the benefit of the intellectual or Realist and the Mystic. To understand my beliefs, we must first understand the basics of most other popularized forms of Satanism.

Part 1-A Laveyan Satanism and Authoritarianism

Let us begin with Lavey's and companies Philosophy. Most of the COS splinter groups follow the same basic philosophy, except for minor organizational differences. They believe in what I call Puritan Individualism, which is total Self-Godhood. This means absolutely nothing comes before them, except maybe family and loved ones. There is no core loyalty or benefit of the whole. This is why I call it a mercenary belief system.

They also combine a bit of objectivism into their beliefs, where they believe that they are not victims or that they are not oppressed in anyway. This in a sense denies the reality of forces beyond your control, which have ultimately affected a greater percentage of the outcome of your achievements in your lifetime. I don't believe in all of the concepts of objectivism.

Laveyan philosophy is against all organized religion, which reveals their own business like hypocrisy. This cult of atheists has no real religious message or higher goals to attain. They therefore, stand against the simplest idealism, the same idealism that has raised society up out of the depths of human chaos and misguided confusion, and laveyans are without any real goals to rise up and achieve! Though, laveyan Satanists do accept the need to embrace those fantasy ideals in their rituals as long as they do not ultimately sink into a nonsensical belief that denies the carnal fulfillment of Man and Woman.

Through fantasy we fulfill a psychological need. This I agree with, but why confine those ideals to our rituals alone? If Satanism is fulfillment, then why not indulge in the pleasures of our Idealistic Fantasies on a full-time basis?

Maybe the ancients, who were not nonsensical, did this very thing. To me fantasy and reality are very close and sometimes one can not be determined from the other. If something can not be proved or disproved, it is a fantasy, but it can never be denied from reality completely.

Part 1-B Laveyan Satanism and Authoritarianism

So, believing in such fantasy beliefs can do no harm directly as long as we realize that they are never an absolute truth, but merely our personal truths! Therefore, no group, order, or religion, has the right to enforce all of their beliefs, moral-values, etc., upon other people, groups, etc. This would infringe upon the Natural Spiritual Rights of others, which again laveyian objectivism opposes and means they believe that there are no natural rights at all. This includes primeval rights as opposed to Spiritual Rights, the only thing I do agree with.

As primeval creatures, we had no rights, but we have evolved, through our spiritual ideals, creating society and higher civilization, based upon natural foundational spiritual rights. Many groups, religions go beyond the foundational basics and create laws to enforce all of their moral-values, even upon people of opposing moral-values which harm no others. christianity totally enforces their moral-values, beliefs, etc., upon others through civil laws, that oppresses billions and creates a nonsensical belief system, which goes against human nature and our carnal fulfillment, as would any other belief system that rises to such fanaticism.

So, laveyan satanists can not argue about judeo-christianities nonsensical beliefs, which makes them sound like a victim to me, through their belief that there are no true natural rights. The purpose of society is to secure humanities Spiritual Rights and raise us from the jungle. Some where humanity took a wrong turn down the road of nonsensical (non-carnal) religion. They also didn't fully realize the science that I'm now revealing to you, which only effects living beings and will eternally transcend our idealistic spiritual beliefs, polluting our Spiritual Society with the Natural Scientific Laws of Dominion!

They are scientific because they can be proven beyond a shadow of a doubt. This means they are purely realistic/materialistic, not spiritual or fantasy bound. These laws need to be incorporated into the very foundations of the schools of society and used to benefit our society.

These laws are and have always been incorporated into the natural world and our societies, but I doubt that they were always taught and used in the erecting of society. These 4 principles reveal the authoritarian nature of animal society. These are the principles we all use, most unknowingly and will always affect our lives. These are the Natural Authoritarian Laws that all organizations use to dominate their enemies. These are the laws christianity uses to oppress us, through their moral-value system transformed into civil laws. Therefore, I'm not against these true natural laws. This means I believe in fighting fire with fire. We will defeat judeo-christianity through Counter-Authoritarianism! This does not mean we will force them to believe in our principles, it just means we will take back our Spiritual (Religious) Rights through the true Laws of Nature! This is what I mean by saying that Satanism must become a real religion and not some false religion, an anti-religion.

1. Dominate or be Dominated.
2. Strength in Numbers.
3. New and Better Knowledge always prevails over Old and Useless Knowledge.
4. Order controls Chaos.

Part 2 Traditional Satanism
And
The Philosophy of 999

There have been many so-called Satanic groups over the years, but very few were actually Satanic in the christian sense, but were of course deemed so through christian beliefs. Most of these groups and religions were in existence before christianity or sprung up around the same time as the foundation of christianity and were undoubtedly rivals for power and control.
Christianity, made it very clear that they were the dominant authoritarian power through its whole extermination and destruction of peoples, cultures, religions, and their histories. Some of these Groups and Religions were the Cathars, Luciferians, Waldensians, and even the Knights Templars who combined Mithraism with christianity, etc.
Later on, there were other groups like the english Hell-Fire Club and then Dashwood's Hell-Fire Club. The motto of the club was borrowed from Rabelais, "Fay Ce Que Voudras!" This means, Do What You Will! This is very similar to Crowley's Motto, "There Is No Grace, There Is No Guilt. This Is The Law, Do What Thou Wilt!" I think Crowley borrowed it as well!
The term Traditional Satanist, has come to mean a Satanist that believes in more Traditional Satanic Philosophies, Religions, etc. The main aspect of these so-called Traditional beliefs is a belief in and worshipping of the actual christian devil and the evil that it represents.
In my opinion, there are very few if any Truly Traditional Groups in existence and therefore these Satanists and Traditional Satanic Groups are actually contemporary or modern groups, a name which Lavey has popularized for His own adopted beliefs.

In reality, all of these groups and different denominations are truly representative of Contemporary Satanic Groups and Beliefs, including all of these foolish pagan groups as well! My Philosophy of The 999 brings us to my beliefs, which ultimately combine aspects of all these Contemporary Satanic Beliefs. This means it's a combination of so-called Contemporary Satanism and so-called Traditional Satanism!

My Satan is the Deity and Divinity of Creation. We are a part of Creation and therefore, we are the Lesser Deities/Divinities of Creation. Within all of Creation, the duality exists and also the dueling of Creation. This Creation has a Dark Force and a Light Force, a Masculine Force, and a Feminine Force, a Positive Force, and a Negative Force. As a product of Creation, we are a reflection of this Androgynous Creation and therefore we are Androgynous Beings, Naturally Bisexual and physically separated as Man and Woman, the Duality of Creation.

I believe that the number nine represents not only the end of a cycle, but the beginning as well. This is the Greek Alpha and the Omega!

This is symbolic of Completion and represents the eternal cycle of life and death and of Creation itself. Therefore, it is a sacred number of Creation and Spirituality/Religion. I use three nines to symbolically represent My Holy Trinity of Satan.

The nine in the center represents Androgynous Creation, our God/Goddess and the New Completed Religion. It is completed because after each resurrection of society from the ashes of imperfection and uselessness, it is finally rising in a state of perfection, The Golden Phoenix!!! The nine to the right represents Man and His Conservatism. The nine to the left represents Woman and Her Liberalism. Together they fulfill the Divine Marriage and represent a state of Balance and Resurrection Achieved!!! This is My Mysticism, My Reality and Fantasy! This is My Androgynous Creation, My Bisexual God/Goddess! This is My Satan, My-Self!

Part 3 Vampir Satanism 999
And
Satan's Vampir Knights

The whole concept of Vampir Satanism begins with the belief that Life or Creation is Vampiric in nature, from the beginning. This is the concept of Life feeding on Life to survive!

Therefore, we are all born Vampir and don't truly require the assistance of another Vampir to become a Vampir. Though, this is done very symbolically and is representative of Sacred Initiation!

Blood is a Divinely Sacred Symbol in the world of Vampirism, representing the source and Power of all Life, Immortal Life!

Vampirism may stand on its own as a religion, just like Satanism may stand on its own as a way of Life. Though, I feel that Vampirism becomes a true religion when combined with the principles of a true religion.

Therefore, Vampirism combined with my Satanism 999, becomes Vampir Satanism 999 as recognized through my Satanic Vampir Creed! There is also the aspect of the Sorcerer and the Warrior that is combined here. Since, the original meaning of a Vampir was a type of Sorcerer and we can say that their Power is attained through their Blood and others Blood. This is like kundalini, chi, tao, or the dao, etc.

This is also the same as the force in the sci-fi stories of Star Wars and is the Power of The Martial Artist. This Power must be perfected through Purification. The Blood must be Pure! This leads to the Art of Alchemy and the foundation of The Martial Temple of Satanic Vampir Knights!!!

This Priestly Order has Four Degrees of Mastery:
1. The Vampir/ess, The Initiate.
2. Priest/ess, The First Degree of Mastery.
3. Priest/ess, The Second Degree of Mastery.
4. Androgynist, The Ultimate Degree of Mastery.

Part II Church Orders

Satan's Vampir Knights

Purpose and Goal

Welcome Satanic Vampires! I am an Ordained Priest and the sole founder of this infant order. I like to call myself The First Priest, instead of High Priest. I hope you've enjoyed some of my esoteric spiritual scriptures. If you didn't, maybe this path isn't for you. I don't expect you to take them all literally, just with a sense of spiritual awareness. Yes, this is a path of spirituality, as well as materialism. Like many, I believe in a balance and maintaining that balance. To me, the essence and heart of the mind, is the soul. This is my balance, the spiritual and material, mental and physical. I consider myself a Warrior-Priest. Therefore, this is the path of the Spiritual Warrior, The Martial Way. I have decided on using a simple military ranking system. This system corresponds to my ideals and appeals to my sense of order and sophistication. Everyone starts out weak and will grow stronger or die. Out of this process, we have visualized and made our path. This was and always shall be the ultimate goal, improvement of the self. If during this process, we happen to change the world, then so be it!

Training

If you decide to join my temple, your training will begin immediately. You will be tested for your physical health and strength. In addition, you will also be tested for your intelligence and knowledge. Therefore, your training will consist of two branches, the mental/spiritual and the physical/material. As the guardians of the temple, we will be prepared mentally and physically, to stave off attack, from our enemies!

Mental/Spiritual

Your knowledge of religion and spirituality, will help to mold and perfect your greater personality and spiritual awareness. Your personality and spiritual awareness in turn effects your physical health and vice versa. This is where your knowledge of spiritual healing, will benefit you and others. This knowledge will transcend to actual physical healing. All of this is necessary, for you are to be a Warrior-Priest or Warrior-Priestess. Eventually, we hope to reach out to other branches of knowledge, to offer an alternative mental path.

Physical/Material

Your physical training will help maintain your physical health and again, vice versa. Remember that the body is our temple! We must purify the temple with clean water and fresh air. So, we try to eliminate poisons and toxins from our bodies and from entering our bodies in the first place. We do this because these poisons and toxins will contaminate us and cause mental and physical illness. Therefore, we will combine the use of proper nutrition and regimented exercise, to maintain maximum health. This will be achieved through the development of our spiritual health consciousness.

Rank and File

Rank is something very sacred that must be earned righteously and honorably! As your progress grows, you will be tested, along the way.
If you pass your tests, you will be granted the proper Rank and privileges. I expect you, to do your best, climbing The Mountain of Glory!

Satan's Vampir Healers

This is The Order of The Sacred Sexual/Spiritual Healers! This Order is made up of three classes of Healers. Each class is separated by the degree or level of healing that they perform.

Whether or not they charge a fee for their services is their personal and sacred right and no one will take this sacred right away from them without facing the Knights and Soldiers of this Church Of The Antichrist. These Sacred Priests and Priestesses are the Holy Whores of Babylon or the Divine Prostitutes that support the foundation of Our New World Economy. Through their Sacred Work, we shall fill the Golden Vaults of Babylon once again and raise Our Holy Order from judeo-christian oppression to the Final and Glorious Seats of Judgment. Hail The Holy Whore! Hail The Sacred Prostitute! Hail the Church Of The Antichrist!

Satan's Vampir Army

This military institution is the main body and vanguard of our movement. This organization is a separate entity, from Satan's Vampir Knight's of The Temple! The Knights are an elite order, The Priestess/Priesthood, devoted to serving and protecting Satan's Divine Vampir Temple! Though, everyone who joins the Church of The Antichrist is automatically considered a Warrior-Priest/Priestess, a royally devout soldier of The Ideal Antichrist! Our Militia is an order dedicated to protecting The Satanic Vampir People! Therefore, this is The People's Satanic Vampir Army! This citizens' militia and the Knights are sworn to live by and uphold the values of Satan's Divine Vampir Bible and The Satanic Vampir Creed! Beyond those values, there will be very few mandates for the militia, unlike those that the Knights must adhere to. One of your other jobs as a soldier will be to recruit new members into our organization. You will be given a monetary commission for each new member that you bring into our organization. Therefore, this is one way that you can benefit by being a member of our organization. If you become an agent for us today, tomorrow you will definitely profit!

Part III Church Principles

The Virtuous Principles of Satanism 999

1. **Allegiance**
2. **Brotherhood/Sisterhood**
3. **Truth/Respect**
4. **New World Order**
5. **Sexual Freedom**
6. **Life**

1. **Allegiance** represents duty and becomes, "The Grand Responsibility of The True Nobility!"
2. **Brotherhood and Sisterhood** represents love and strength, which becomes, "The Apocalyptic Embracement of Hatred!"
3. **Truth and Respect** represents honor and integrity, becoming, "The Sacred Acceptance!"
4. **New World Order** represents new world religion, rebirth, youth, and beauty, becoming, "The Divine Resurrection!"
5. **Sexual Freedom** represents release, relief, and fulfillment, becoming, "The Realization and Spiritual Enlightenment of The Holy Union!"
6. **Life** represents triumph and immortality, which is, "The Providential Existence!"

Prologue Part 1 The Solution

I do not have to receive an orthodox education, to be an intelligent, knowledgeable, Priest and Healer! I especially, do not have to be a clean-cut conformist, dressed in a monkey-suit, to be a professional! I am a mystic Warrior-Priest! I call my belief system Vampir Satanism 999, The Antichrist Solution! Through my religion, I offer social, economic, and religious salvation, to my Satanic Brothers and Sisters! Nine Nine Nine, is Satan's Divine Trinity! Nine is the end of a cycle and the end symbolizes the beginning. Therefore, Nine is a divine number, representing the beginning and the end, the alpha and the omega! This is the number of my androgynous Goddess/God! Men and Women are one with creation and so we are our own individual lesser Goddesses and Gods! This means Nine is also the number of Woman and Man! Through the Divine Marriage, we become one and so three Nines represent our oneness! The middle Nine represents, our Goddess/God and the New Religion! The Nine to the right represents, Man and his Conservatism! The Nine to the left represents, Woman and her Liberalism! Together, the three Nines represent Balance and Resurrection!

Prologue Part 2 The Sign

I have chosen this hexagram as my personal seal! This hexagram is a symbol that represents the greater consciousness of creation, in the macrocosm and the lesser consciousness of the human psyche, in the microcosm! Therefore, this symbol of creation represents my great androgynous Goddess/God and the lesser Goddess/Gods, Men and Women! Since we are a part of creation, we realize our oneness, with creation itself! This is the Divine Union or Divine Marriage, between Brother and Sister, and our androgynous Goddess/God! I have tattooed this talismanic symbol of creation upon my forehead, so that others can see it and bare witness, as it is a sign of initiation into a New Religious Order! Through initiation, it becomes a symbol of devotion, which means sacrifice! I am founding this Order as its first initiate, self-baptized, as The Avenger, The First Priest of Satan's Divine Vampir Temple! I now reveal to the world, my New Moral-Value System! Behold, "Satan's Divine Vampir Bible!" This is our true book of revelation, free and devoid of foundational hypocrisy, institutional dogma, and unwarranted bias! I am The Apostle of Satan and the time is now!

Prologue Part 3 My Fantasy

What I believe is my fantasy! There is no truth here, but my truth! My real God is Myself! No one can say to me that is dogma! Everyone is a hypocrite, especially me! If you say, I'm not a hypocrite then you are a lying hypocrite! This book contains my Moral-Value System! No one can say this system or that system is the right system, which is institutionalized dogma! This system is for those who believe in it! My goal is to dethrone, the judeo-christian Moral-Value System! No system should have authority over the whole! If it does, then you have been subjugated by that very religion, its leaders, and the believers or followers of that religion! This means church and state/federal authority is only partially severed on a legal level and not at all, on an ethical level! If we are going to have separation, we must have a true, total, and complete separation of church and state/federal authority! Otherwise, each state must have the power to authorize and dictate its own ethical standards and policies!

Let me introduce you to, The Satanic State! This will be the state, within the state, the power, within the power! Through my state authority, we shall completely overthrow, the judeo-christian Moral-Value System! Hail Satan!

The Moral of Allegiance

Everyone who believes in their society is responsible for their society, just as much as it is responsible for you, because your society exists to serve you, the loyal people! This means your society must provide all physical and psychological needs that are essential to your continuing health. Therefore, you will prove your true allegiance, through your duty, the work you must do. If your society cannot provide everyone with work, then those governing your society are at fault, not the people, because of lack of employment. If you are proven unhealthy and incapable of working, you will be granted impunity. If there is opportunity for employment and you are perfectly capable of working and you still choose not to work, then you are guilty of disloyalty, non-allegiance! For this crime, these people will be deported from the state or penalized into a work force program, to attain maximum efficiency. Allegiance is the heart of all great societies and when it is completely lost, so is the society. Ultimately, "The Grand Responsibility of The True Nobility," is the duty each of us must perform, revealing the depths of our great allegiance. Allegiance is the moral glue, holding together our sacred Brotherhood and Sisterhood. We must cherish our moral of allegiance, for it is the life blood and foundation, raising up our social temple, The New Satanic State!

The Moral of Brotherhood
and
Sisterhood

From time to time, the people of the world have captured the true essence of the family structure. Our great family structure includes aspects of idealistic/spiritualistic and materialistic/realistic codes that make it a solid, worthy structure. This means there are no cracks, weak spots, or holes, no Achilles heel that can be penetrated, by enemies of the state. Allegiance is the bloodline of the Brotherhood and Sisterhood, which reveals our true love, giving our family structure its strength, rising to defeat all opposition in the final earth war, "The Apocalyptic Embracement of Hatred!" Everyone must embrace their hate, accepting it, understanding who and why you are! Through this you'll know what you believe in and for who do you stand? Do you stand for or against, The Apostle of Satan? I say, love your loyal Brothers and Sisters, and hate disloyalty!

The Moral of Truth and Respect

Truth and Respect work side by side. Without Truth, there is no Respect and vice versa! If there is no Truth or Respect, there is no Love, no Allegiance, and no Brotherhood or Sisterhood!

Through our moral of Truth and Respect, we gain personal and public honor and integrity. All of us seek acceptance in one form or another, becoming a psychological and physical goal as with all The Satanic Morals. This ultimately leads us to "The Sacred Acceptance!" The Sacred Acceptance is learning to accept people of all race and sexuality into The New State. However, this excludes people promoting and supporting all religions representing the judeo-christian Moral-Value System! These religions are hypocritical, biased, and dogmatized, claiming that their principles are the only moral truth, yet it is only their truth! Through this claim, people with different moral principles are mocked, degraded, and made outcasts of free society?

The peoples' government adopted its formal system of ethics from a dominating religious majority. This was a christian majority, enforcing its rule, even though church and state authority, had supposedly been severed, long ago? What this means, is that we are still ruled by, christian authoritarianism, through religious/political intervention! This in turn outcasts even more people because of authoritarian laws made according to those adopted ethics. These laws should not exist and shall cease to exist in "The New Satanic State!"

"We shall break the whip of oppression, swallowing the lords of christian society and the tumultuous masses of right-wing masochists, spreading, The Satanic Temple, to the four corners of the earth!!!"

The Moral of A New World Order

All of us, seek youth and beauty, the symbols of perfection. So the old becomes a symbol of uselessness and imperfection, driving us toward new and better creations. Through our longing for these new and better creations, we arrive at a great spiritual rebirth, through a New World Religion. This new world religion timelessly erects a New World Order through "The Divine Resurrection!" For the old isn't truly destroyed, only reborn, and redesigned, better than before, insuring us with new hope, new faith, and new allegiance! All of these beliefs and ideals help bring us toward the acceptance of The New Phoenix rising from its ashes of uselessness and imperfection! Behold The Perfected One, Resurrected, bringing forth the principles of The New World Religion, Vampir Satanism 999!!!

The Moral of Sexual Freedom

Sexual freedom means just that, the freedom of any willing adult to engage in sexual relations with any other willing adult without discrimination or condemnation. This is the absolute acceptance of a person's sexuality, be it heterosexual, homosexual, or bisexual, etc. This person's sexuality also includes whether or not they are abstinent or promiscuous, polygamous or monogamous, permanently cohabiting, or even a soliciting prostitute! We shall never accept moral judgment, based upon sexual behavior, only true character! The release of our sexual anxieties brings us relief and fulfillment of our sexual desires. Through this we are freed of possible deeper more complex psychological disorders caused by sexual repression. Our moral of Truth and Respect guides us with "The Sacred Acceptance!" of all anti-christian people toward, "The Realization and Spiritual Enlightenment of The Holy Union!" The Holy Union is The Divine Marriage between ourselves in our Brotherhood and Sisterhood to our androgynous Goddess/God of creation. For we are all one!
"Then when the Goddess/God finally awoke from its sleep, mortality was just a dream, slowly forgotten!"
"**Satan** is the father of truth and the mother of desire. Lies are only beliefs until they are proven false and the will, only control, until dethronement by a superior power. For christianity, will be overthrown by, The Masters' of The Black Arts!"
"**Homosexuality** breaks through the veils of pseudo-christian purity and frees the androgynous nature of Man and Woman. For the true God is unmasked in the souls of Men and Women, through the freedom of expression, especially, sexual expression!" **Satan's Sorcery-Volume I**

The Moral of Life

Life is a magnificently divine phenomenon, echoing through an eternal saga, climaxing out of our flight from Death in the ultimate triumph, Immortality! From our Sacred Marriage to the Goddess/God we are spiritually enlightened to our own God and Goddess-hood. Through this we realize our potential for escaping Death becoming literal Gods and Goddesses. This motivational potential is the divine fuel or divine power that will finally escalate humanity into "The Providential Existence!" The Phoenix rises, dressed anew, with golden feathers as we bless Her for our cosmic voyage. She is purified, baptized through fire. This is an initiation and the inauguration of a New Golden Age! Fly with me, loyal Brothers and Sisters. Fly with me, to the heavens!!! I am your Avenger, The Apostle of Satan!!!

"If you want disciples, follow yourself! If you want lovers, love yourself! If you want truth, believe in yourself! If you want Life, Live!!!" **Satan's Sorcery Volume II**

Part IV Church Regulations

Antichrist Blacklist

1. Boy Scouts of America
We are hereby blacklisting the "Boy Scouts of America" and all other organizations, which associate and support them and their beliefs! They are a christian organization, which has publicly denounced and condemned the beautiful, legitimate, and growing lifestyle of homosexuality!

2. Roman Catholic Church
We are hereby blacklisting the "Roman Catholic Church" and all its protestant fissures! The church has stood as a blockade to true moral freedom, for far too many centuries. They have killed millions in the name of god and christ. They have outcast the innocent and destroyed truly advanced knowledge. They have stood as a front for organized crime and acted as true blood sucking vampires, draining their own people of their precious and hard earned wealth. Therefore, they have grown fat and arrogant in the name of god, while three quarters of the people of the world still live in absolute destitute. The people of the world have been forced into a totally preventable calamity, known as poverty, by their very own religious/political leaders. You might think after two thousand years, if they were altruistic or divine, that poverty would not exist, gays and prostitutes would be respected and loved for their true character, that they would not egotistically claim to possess the only true god and the only true moral-value system. The roman catholic church will be leveled to the ground by my sword of truth, my new moral-value system!

3. U.S. Military
We are hereby blacklisting all branches of the "U.S. Military!" They have come a long way when it comes to equal rights for women, but their hypocritically shifty attitude toward homosexuality has deemed them unworthy and unsupportive

proponents of gay rights, thereby warranting blacklist status! They obviously are representing and supporting right-wing christian moral-values! A point to military command. We want you to remember The Greek Army, because they conquered most of the world! Fear The Gay Army! NO GUTS, NO GLORY!!! (Note: On Sept. 20, 2011 Don't Ask Don't Tell was repealed and we hope this brings an end to the right-wing homophobic bias in the military. Our blacklist has ended, but we will keep this here as an important reminder for those who want to secure and maintain their rights!)

Birth-Rights or The Right To Life

1. The Right to Live Free in your own personal environment!
2. The Right to Fulfill All of your Reasonable Desires and Needs!
3. The Right to Destroy your Oppressor!
4. The Right to Attain Possessions!
5. The Right to Believe what You Will!

You're only a servant, never a slave, until you say and believe that you have no rights! You have the rights to live free and to fulfill your reasonable desires! If you are not free and cannot legally fulfill your reasonable desires, you have become an oppressed servant of the ruling power! In reality, you are a slave to the dominant force, though spiritually you'll never be a real slave if you believe in your personal rights as a living being! You have The Birth-Rights or The Rights To Life, so don't ever let anyone tell you, that you have no rights! For at that moment, you'll become a slave to the higher ruling power and to those who deceive you by telling you such lies and nonsense!

Sacred Regulations
Of
Satan's Vampir Knights

1. All Warrior-Priest/ess must complete the Secret Regulation!
2. All Warrior-Priest/ess must keep their heads shaven as a sign of initiation and sacrifice!
3. All Warrior-Priest/ess must not use drugs or alcohol, only sparingly during sacred ritual upon the Greater or Lesser Sabbath, The Great Saturnalia, Saturday, and other selected holy days!
4. All Warrior-Priest/ess must join one more creditable Satanic, Vampir, or Thelemaic organization!
5. All Warrior-Priest/ess must study religion, magick, and the occult in general!
6. All Warrior-Priest/ess must train in at least one form of martial art!
7. All Warrior-Priest/ess must eat healthy nutritious diets, including regular and regimented daily exercise!
8. All Warrior-Priest/ess must have a healthy amount of deep sleep and REM sleep each day!

Satan's Vampir Knights

Basic Rules of Ministry

1. Satan's Ministers will obey all commands of The Supreme Master, The High Priest and General of The Legion or face expulsion; excommunication! For Satanism 999, represents absolute Allegiance!
2. Satan's Ministers will not preach against, mock, or defame other Ministers of Satan's Divine Vampir Temple! For Satanism 999, represents true Brotherhood and Sisterhood!
3. Satan's Ministers will not lie to their Disciples! For Satanism 999, represents Truth and Respect!
4. Satan's Ministers will not support judeo-christianity in any way or form! For Satanism 999, represents The New World Order!
5. Satan's Ministers will not preach against or mock any form of sexual expression that occurs between advocates, through their own free will! For Satanism 999, represents all Sexual Freedom!
6. Satan's Ministers will not preach suicide and death as a solution, unless the circumstances are unbearable and horrifying; then it will be an escape from torturous, degrading, miserable existence! For Satanism 999, represents Life in all its magnificence!

The 4 Crowned Pillars

The Four Crowned Pillars of the Church Of The Antichrist include:

1. Faith
2. Will
3. Work
4. Knowledge

All of these are to be adopted and used with equal respect to the other. Through this combination or formula we shall maintain and spread Our Superior Order of Vampir Satanism 999!

1. In Our Faith is Belief, which is what raises us out of bed each morning or night, with hopes and dreams of fulfillment. If we lose Faith, we lose sight of Our Lesser and Greater Physical and Spiritual Goals and Our Hearts are weakened. We must constantly renew Our Faith, with personal forms of Initiation and Vows of Loyalty, which MUST BE HONORED! Faith is the complement of Will!
2. Our Will is Our Ultimate Strength to Rise Above all blockades and Overcome them and Our Enemies! Through Super-Will The Sorcerer becomes a Great Master and an Organization becomes Invincible! You will all Learn The Power of Conviction! Will is the complement of Work!
3. Our Work is what we Convict Ourselves to every day. We must be steadfast and determined to complete Our Work. When you Work, you must do it with that Conviction and do it as Best as You Can or it will be Worthless and a sign of Weakness. Everything that we do for Our Society, Our People must be

Honored and considered Sacred Work. Work is the complement of Knowledge!

4. Our Knowledge is the Final Crowned Pillar in this Formula of Success. Our Knowledge is built into Our Work and becomes the foundation of all that we Stand For. The Super-Human Children of tomorrow will hold this Knowledge in their Hands as a Great Trophy, a Reward and a Symbol of Humanities Eternal Sacrifice, looking back at Civilizations Devotion to Rising Out of The Primeval Pit of Mortality and Suffering!

Humankind Will Triumph in The End and Humanity will say, We have Won the War against False Religion such as christianity, Suffering such as disease, and Governmental Failures such as Primitive Capitalism! This Knowledge will be a Crystal Key to The Fortress of Humanity and it is All Powerful and as Divine as Ourselves and Our Faith! Knowledge is therefore the complement of Faith!

The Antichrist Soldier's Rules of Conduct

1. Chain of Command
The Antichrist Soldier, recognizes the Chain of Command! Insubordination is a sign of internal weakness and the lack of higher discipline. Your enemies will see your lack of self-control and your disorganization, capitalizing on your pathetic weaknesses. What is a Militia without Order and Control?

2. Engagement of The Enemy
The Antichrist Soldier, will never engage the enemy, unless Ordered by a Superior Officer or in Self-Defense. This means directly and literally, never to inflict bodily harm or to damage any property of the enemy, without Official Authorization! What good will you be as a Soldier, when you're in jail and costing us billions of dollars?

3. Uniform Compliance
The Antichrist Soldier, will comply with the Uniform Codes, while Officially on Duty. What will the enemy think, when you come before them dressed up and looking like a slob, and a lazy maggot? They will mock you, laughing at your inferior qualities and sense of duty, reflected upon your obvious half-hearted insincerity! Are you for real or are you a joke? How serious are you???

4. Satanic Camaraderie
The Antichrist Soldier, accepts the principles of Satan's Divine Vampir Bible, A New Moral-Value System and The Satanic Vampir Creed! These Satanic Morals are designed to preserve Our Unity, help raise and maintain Our Morale, and manifest our Undying Unified Spirit! One is the beginning! What is the key that makes Our Unity Superior, to other organizations???

Church Of The Antichrist 999 Handbook

Part 1 The Order of Satan's Vampir Soldiers

Once you join the Church Of The Antichrist you are automatically registered into this Order of Satan's Soldiers with proper rank. One of your jobs is to help recruit new members and you can apply for Official Recruiter or Circle Master Status which has many benefits. Your other great job is to help defend the Church Of The Antichrist and our Satanic Brothers and Sisters!

This is a solitary order that works together through the leaders of the circles in your areas. This Order is not too religious, though it is mainly for those who wish to support our Church yet have no desire to become deeply involved with aspects of spirituality or Priest/Priestesshood. Though, after a long list of members who kept inquiring about a solitary Priest/Priestess Status among the Warrior Class I've decided to allow Priest/Priestesshood to flourish in this solitary order. All those who are interested in that Status must apply for it.

Each Official Recruiter becomes the head of their own Circle, a Circle Master, with the rank of an Officer! They can now recruit members into their Circle, which is a smaller branch of The Order of Satan's Soldiers, a Larger Branch of the Church Of The Antichrist. Each new member that you bring into your Circle will be used to value your worth and to elevate your Official Rank! As the Head of a Circle, you get to name your Circle whatever you like, though it must be authorized as your Official Name. If you apply for Priest/Priestess Status, you will be given the title High Priest or High Priestess, along with your standard military rank. All those that you recruit into your Circle will be given the title Priest or Priestess, along with their rank.

Part 2 The Order of Sacred Sexual Vampir Healers

After joining the Church Of The Antichrist you will have the choice of joining this solitary order or our Elite Order of Satan's Vampir Knights! Your main job in this Order is to find those who are in need of sexual fulfillment and bring them into your Circle of Sexual Worship!

You may apply for head status becoming High Priestess or High Priest of your Circle or you may join a Circle. If you join a Circle you will be given the title Priest/Priestess with your military rank. Those at the head will also be promoted to a status of Officer! The High Priest or High Priestess may use whatever spiritually/mentally emotional or materialistically/physically fulfilling arts that they wish, as long as the tenets of my Satanic Bible are followed. They can teach these methods to the members of their Circle.

Again, as the head of your Circle as Circle Master, you can name it what you will, yet it must be authorized as your Official Name! The Sacredness of this order must be emphasized and not forgotten. You are providing a service to The Satanic People, because Sexuality is more than a desire, it is a NEED that must be fulfilled in order for a Human Being to be healthy. Also, since you are providing such a great service to Humanity, you must be Honored, Respected, and Glorified! Hail The Holy Whores' of Babylon!

Part 3 The Order Of Satan's Vampir Knights

After joining the Church Of The Antichrist you will also have a choice of joining this Order. This is the Elite Order of Satan's Knights of Valor or The Knights of The Temple! This Order is dedicated to defending the Temple itself and protecting, teaching, and spreading the Sacred Principles of my Satanic Bible.

This is an Order of Warrior-Priests and Warrior-Priestesses. We not only train in The Martial Arts, we train in the Religious/Magickal Arts and The Official Arts and Ceremonial Rites of this Temple. Since, this is an Elite order, there is only one High Priest or First Priest and that is myself. Also, all rules must be followed completely or excommunication from the Church Of The Antichrist will ensue or expulsion from this Order! This also, is a very Sacred Order. The members of this Order hold the highest Honor, Respect, and Glory and must be shown such Respect, Honor, and Glory! As for applying for Circle Master Status, you will be given the title Vice-High Priest or Vice-High Priestess! Special rules apply and other initiative rank and titles will be used as well.

Part 4 Circle Master
Application Regulations

1. You must serve one year in a Circle, before you can apply for Circle Master Status!
2. You must have at least five members ready to join your Circle or have five join in one month!
3. You must either have Officer Status or be accepted and granted Officer Status!
4. You must have or build your own website promoting the Church Of The Antichrist!
5. If you fail these rules you must wait one year before reapplying for Circle Master Status!

The Definitions of A Satanist 999

1. You must support the complete overturning of the judeo-christian moral-value system! This makes you a true adversary of judeo-christianity. The ancient semitic word for adversary or opponent is Satan! Therefore, as a true adversary, you come as a true Satan against them!
2. You must support My New Left-Hand Path Moral-Value System, The Philosophy of 999! This creates balance and stabilization where there is confusion, destabilization, imbalance, and emptiness, filling the void!
3. You must support Satanism 999 as a real Religion and not some pseudo-anti-religion! Satanism must become Satanism 999! As a real religion, you must accept Satan as a real divinity within yourself or creation! Therefore, you must accept the term Satanist 999!
4. You must support the formal organization of Satanism 999, within the Church of The Antichrist! This is the formal organization of a legitimate Priest and Priestess-hood, dedicated to Satanism 999, as an actual dignified religion! This formalization will give Satanism 999 a true and solid foundation to build upon and grow! This excludes other organizations that may work against the goals of the Church of The Antichrist! Through a solid foundation I swear that Satanism 999 will have a long future ahead and we will be freed from judeo-christian oppression!
5. You must support all Left-Wing concepts and principles set forth by the Church of The Antichrist! This excludes all right-wing judeo-christian concepts and principles! Many of these Left-Wing principles include the true natural rights to gay

marriage, gays in the military, prostitution, pandering, drugs, abortion, capital punishment, etc.! (Note: This is actually a combination of left and right but leans more to the left. Some of these principles may change depending upon how I view them later on in life. I may be willing to debate capital punishment, depending upon the circumstances.)

The Precepts of Salvation

1. Life is always greater than death, unless death is escape and freedom from living hell!
2. Divine Family is always greater than common family and self, unless Divine Family takes away your true freedom!
3. Health is always greater than wealth or money and power, unless wealth secures your Health!
4. Peace is always greater than war, unless war is unavoidable and it is a last resort to securing true freedom and Eternal Peace!
5. Spirit is always greater than law, when law has stolen your true rights and freedom, unless Spirit allows law to exist!
6. Love is always greater than hate, unless hate must rise in war!
7. One Unity is always greater than many, unless One enslaves your true rights!
8. Sexuality is always greater than abstinence, unless abstinence assumes your Sexuality!
9. Discipline is always greater than rebellion, unless rebellion is the true path to Higher Discipline!
10. Purity is always greater than toxins and contamination, unless contamination leads you out of contamination into Eternal Purity!
11. Truth is always greater than lies, unless lies reveal the Truth!
12. Calm is always greater than anger, unless anger brings Ultimate Calm!
13. Idolization and Worship of The Self is always greater than outside deities, unless Idolization of outside deities represent Idolization of The Self!

The Satanic Vampir Creed

1. Beauty
The Satanic Vampir endeavors to remain forever beautiful, yet beauty is always seen through, The Eye of The Beholder! It will be the task of the Vampir to use its power, by creating an alluring aura, which is the beauty of the true Sorcerer. What is within can be seen from without!
Beauty is Youth, Beauty is Power, Beauty is Wisdom, Beauty is Art, Beauty is Soul, Beauty is Lust, Beauty is Triumph, Beauty is Parade, Beauty is Immortality!
2. Anti-Regret
The Satanic Vampir should stand by its own ideals, never to regret its thoughts or actions, but to always face the ax of self-deceit, when sympathy is born! Don't slaughter the lambs and then pity them, out of pseudo-innocence and visual aesthetics.
3. Power
The Satanic Vampir seeks out power for itself and its own or its family, never kneeling to the whims of mortals; the others and will face death, rather than be forced into eternal servitude! If it serves, it serves out of its own desire or necessity. There will always be a master, yet it is better to serve in hell, than to reign in heaven! Choose well your Master or it will choose well you!
4. Lust
The Satanic Vampir must eternally feed, fulfilling its unrelenting sexual lust, draining the souls of mortals! By draining the mortal's power, the Vampir consumes their souls. This turns the mortals into Vampirs during the process. All great Vampir tales are filled with blood feeding, representing a physical desire to sexually embrace the flesh and a deeper sexual desire for the soul, The Life Force!
Therefore, blood is a sacred symbol of sexual existence. Becoming a Satanic Vampir, is not a path to evil, but a path to

immortality. A strong libido represents a great yearning for the sexual life, the sacred and erotic blood of the androgynous sexual soul! This reveals the altruistic and divine nature of Prostitution, Pornography, Polygamy, Promiscuousness, Orgia, Homosexuality, and all other Sacred Sexual Arts!

Part V Church Goals

Antichrist Goals

1. **Sexual Promiscuity**
One goal of the Church of The Antichrist is to replace the Christian family unit, with the sacred polygamous family unit! We frown upon monogamy, because it isolates the partners to each other, cutting off sexual and loving relationships with others. This monogamous greed, denies others of their sexual, loving, and healing pleasures. The future is promiscuousness!

2. **Bisexuality**
Another goal of the Church of The Antichrist is to raise homosexuality and bisexuality to a mainstream status, delegating the heterosexual world to the shadows and memory! We frown upon heterosexuality, because it perpetuates a homophobic bias and fear. This stigma will persist, until the heterosexual is contained and mentally deported, through the power of swaying social conformity. The future is a bisexual society!

3. **Sexual Healing**
Another goal of the Church of The Antichrist is to free the bonds of the holy whore, the Sexual/Spiritual Healer! We frown upon Christian societies damning laws and condemning views of morality. We will establish her profession as the second most sacred ascendancy. She represents Babylon's glorious treasure and we swear to fill the golden vaults. The future is the end of hypocrisy and the beginning of Babylon's glory!

4. **Local Drug Management**
Another goal of the Church of The Antichrist is to create and mandate a new system, to determine the status of controlled substances! The hypocrisy of our society ascends to the top of the mountain of glory and descends to our children. They are caught between the tyrannically puritan values of christianity and greedy rich class politicians and military leaders. They will

wage a pointless and staged war on drugs, knowing they cannot defeat themselves. There are no real benefits except maybe to the politician's career. Any economic benefits are an illusion, because job by job, flush by flush, they are draining your money down the government toilets that ironically cost about $5,000!

Doctors can tell you, the most destructive drug of all to the body, is alcohol and one of the least destructive, a simple herb; which is strangely and ironically labeled, controlled! They should be spending your money on better education and devise a mandate for drug testing in order to regulate its use, to its minimum, eliminating and avoiding most legal hassles. If you mandate drug testing at the job level, you create an ultimate incentive not to use. Did you know for thousands of years, the rich have used drugs to pacify their slaves? Their monopolies will be destroyed, through the breaking of our legal chains. The future is solid and acceptable solutions!

5. The Ascendant State

Another goal of the Church of The Antichrist is to establish ascendancy of state law over federal oppression! We can all see it has proven itself to be a machine of absolute self-interest! The future is ascendancy!

6. Free Energy

Another goal of the Church of The Antichrist is to bring the people free energy, crushing the fossil fuel monopoly. The governments of the world have suppressed and controlled the technologies, which will eliminate our forced-dependence on fossil fuels. The future is, Free Energy!

7. Free Health Care

Another goal of the Church of The Antichrist is to bring the people free health care, destroying the private hospital system and the pseudo-need for insurance! The great irony is, many hospitals are named after christian saints! Plus, millions die, because they cannot afford the drugs they need to survive. The pharmaceutical companies hold the health of the world captive, in their monopolizing grip! Most of these companies are actually owned by greed driven stockholders that could careless about the suffering of others. Here, we are laying the foundation of a truly advanced futuristic society; while they play games in a world of pseudo-luxury, like children at a never-ending party. Though, the party always ends because it is only a temporary luxury. There is nothing wrong with a good party, but we must never forget about the hell that goes on beyond our seemingly invincible paradise. For the poor class, it is always a living hell! So what do the rich do, they make sure there are all kinds of vises to pacify them in their darkest hour. The future is, Free Health Care!

8. Free Housing

Another goal of the Church of The Antichrist is to bring the people, Free Housing! How can the poverty stricken get ahead when they are forced to spend their simple wages on steep rent, instead of better job skills or professional college education? For most, it is mission impossible! How does one escape the trap of poverty? They must have help from their true Brothers and Sisters. The future is, Free Housing!

9. Free Roads

Another goal of the Church of The Antichrist is to bring the people, free roads, eliminating the pseudo-need of tolls and automobile insurance!

10. Free Education

Another goal of the Church of The Antichrist is to bring the people, Free Education! There is no reason why our poverty-stricken children should be forced to work two and three jobs at fast food restaurants, amusement parks, or even join the homosexually biased military, to attain the education which they so dearly deserve, if they truly wish. Is this what capitalist democracy is all about? The education business is an aspiring child's bloody nightmare, unless you're born into the upper class. To make another point, I thought catholicism was here to truly help the people, not drain them of their hard earned wages? So, that is why catholic schools are so expensive; they must be the schools of the rich/ruling class? The future is, Free Education!

11. **Free Food**

Another goal of the Church of The Antichrist is to bring the people, Free Food!

12. **Free Music**

Another goal of the Church of The Antichrist is to bring the people, Free Music! We believe that music is part of the universal language of the soul. Therefore, it is very useful in helping to heal the soul, or the mental mind! The art of spiritual healing has been with us from the beginning, even though it has been suppressed. This is a very wonderful tool that will aide in the process of Spiritual Healing, even physical healing. The problem is that, music is a business which demands a profit. Most of the spiritually sick are very poor and cannot afford the music which will help them feel better. Our Church will consist of many types of healers and will take on the task of bringing Free Healing Music to those who are sick and cannot afford to buy what they truly need! The future is, Free Music!

13. **Free Clothing**

Another goal of the Church of The Antichrist is to bring the people, Free Clothing!

14. **To Secure Our Technological Rights**

Christians are and have banned certain technologies that they feel violates their moral-value or ethical system. These legal bans strip us of our technological rights and oppress us further. They don't recognize our opposing moral-values or our technological rights. It is therefore our goal to fight for, and secure these rights, which will benefit our Great Spiritual Goal of achieving The Providential Existence. We will use every advanced technology in existence, including human cloning, embryonic cloning, stem cell technology, genetic engineering, nano technology, etc., to raise humanity to this super-human state of immortality!

15. **To Secure Our Sexual Rights**

Again Christianity has used its moral-value or ethical system to legally ban certain practices that they find violates their system. Once more, christians don't recognize our opposing moral-values or our Sexual Rights and have stripped us of our rights, oppressing us further. It is our goal to fight for, and secure these rights. Some of them include, gay rights, gays serving openly in the military without discrimination from homophobic military leaders or service men/women, gay marriages on the same level and legal standing as heterosexual couples, polygamy, prostitution, pandering, etc.!

Chart of Organizational Requirements For Advancement

The Essentials

1. The Dream, Idea, Concept, Cause, or Belief
2. The Loyal Supporters
3. The Financial Capital or Equivalent
4. Actual Organizational Development
5. Advanced Technologies

Required Understanding

1. The Supporters must understand that power is the foundational element, to achieve any organizational goals.
2. This power is achieved through economics and politics, via The Political Militia or Political Party.
3. The Supporters must join, donate to, and work for, The Political Militia/Party.
4. The Political Party must be organized like a Militia. You have the Leaders or Officers, the Recruits, Workers, or Soldiers/Supporters.
5. The Officers organize the Party and give out orders and the Soldiers/Supporters carry out the orders and do the work.
6. Many policies must be adopted and complied with to manifest the organization and its goals. So the Supporters must understand that policies are necessary to success.

7. The Supporters must understand absolute dedication to the beliefs and goals is mandatory for success and means dedication to submitting to the work that the Party gives to you to do or complete.

Children of The Machine

We have entered The Age of High Technology! There is no logical reason why the suffering must go on. Who is suffering? Why are they suffering? The poverty stricken are suffering! They are suffering because of the pseudo-elite rich class of the world!
What is the purpose of the current class society? The purpose of the current class society is to maintain the wealth and luxury of the few, rather than the many or at the expense of the many. Every time you support capitalist/democracy, by voting, joining "The Official Military," etc., you support this economic class system. By supporting that system, you empower the rich class and outcast those that are literally forced into poverty, "The Poor Class or Lower Class!"
Those of the rich class have devised a smoke screen, shield, or magic curtain, to hide the unchanging and growing effects of the poverty they enforce upon the majority of the people of the world. They do this through controlling the media, turning activists into terrorists, using covert operations to subdue opposition to their elite order, etc., and when all else fails, they call upon their rich class war machine, "The Official Military!"
What kind of society allows thousands of its people to be laid off without any compensation, by corporations that have just decided to move to a more economically productive location? No true society!
Then what kind of government allows this to occur? A very uncaring and self-motivated government, a corrupt government! There is no true peoples' government; there is only a rich class government!
The Age of The Machine is upon us. The computer now runs society, rather than man. This is a beautiful concept, because a computer cannot be corrupt, only its program. If the rich class

controls the program, then it will be a corrupt machine, a corrupt god. If those of the poor class control the program, the machine will delete the corruption, eliminating poverty!

We are the Children of The Machine and the race has already begun. Our children's children will never know poverty or a corrupt class society! Join the valiant fight, against the true evil! The Dawn of The Apocalypse is here! **Children Of The Machine Unite!** (Evil as in the greater wrong and True as in the closest right!)

Religious Organization and Network

As part of our ever expanding and further development of our Religious Organization and Network, we will need to lay the groundwork for parallel institutions to counter our enemies' sinister clutches on the people of society.

They have been using religious, political/economic, military, medical, psychiatric, psychological, etc., institutions based around religious cores to dominate and oppress everyone with opposing moral-values in this morally/ethically homogenized society that they've created.

Therefore, I am announcing the formation of institutes that will be erected over time to counter every aspect of their oppressive imperialist regime.

We will hereby be organizing The Satanic Religious Association, The Satanic Political/Economic Association, The Satanic Military Association, The Satanic Workers Association, The Satanic Medical Association, and The Satanic Psychiatric/Psychological Association,

The Satanic Artists Association, The Satanic Lawyers Association, Etc.

In these Associations we will gather together many supporters of the beliefs and goals of our Church, uniting them under our banner, working toward the highest social powers and control.

We will also be working on the joint development of The International Satanic League, The Satanic Educational Institute, The Satanic World Peace Party, Etc.

If you would like to participate in the development of any of these organizations that are absolutely necessary, then let us know immediately. Nothing will happen over night! Be prepared for a long drawn out campaign to erect our establishments and to draw any power or control for our uniting people.

We are obviously looking for Satanists/Vampirs, Anti-christians, Politicians, Economists, Trained Officers/Soldiers, Labor Union Bosses/Workers, Medical Doctors, Psychiatrists/Psychologists, Artists/Musicians, Lawyers, Teachers, Scientists, Technicians, Etc.

Sincerely,
Caesar 999

The New World Economy

Welcome to my Church of The Antichrist! Since most of you were a child you were spoon fed two very different tastes, one bitter, the other very sweet.

First the bitter, I'm talking about the right-wing moral-value system of judeo-christianity. This system is undoubtedly on the surface, spiritually representative of the good of the whole or interdependence, which isn't exactly bad by itself. Then they overlap that with an independent social-economic system, the sweet to many especially the rich.

We live in a world economic system, not just a country or national economic system. What we do here affects everyone else in the world.

There is a world economic ladder. In order for the rich to be at the top, the poor must remain at the bottom, which is three quarters of the world! This take care of your own philosophy has allowed the rich or ruling class, to prosper. They have used christianity as an aid to subjugate the masses through religious/political intervention.

Therefore, christianity has always been and always will be a weapon used to attain and stabilize power. It has been the ruling class's ace of spades. The moral-value system itself is meaningless to the ruling class. Hypocrisy can be a King's best friend or worst nightmare.

Though it is essential for them to maintain their weapon, in helping the true christians maintain their moral-value system throughout. The goal of The Church of The Antichrist is to completely overthrow that system, which can't be done without overthrowing those who support and maintain that system!

The first step toward this goal is to understand the greater power of interdependence, which does not mean forgetting our independence.

This only means, we must regard our independence as secondary to the good of the whole in order to accomplish our united goal. Don't think for one moment that this means giving up what you own or the right to owning and running your own business! This simply means, in heart, you know what comes first and you know why! This also means a difference in social/economic policy, but as I said, it doesn't take away, only adding to an imperfect system. This is a start toward a new world economy!

Part VI Church Rituals and Ceremonies

The Holy Initiation: Sacrementum

(This is the sacred initiation oath
of
Satan's Vampir Knights!)

The purpose of my life is Order and to be forever ordained to this Order I have chosen. I am a living sacrifice, for I have dedicated my life to this Order. Since the Creator has vowed to create this Order and has proven so, and has done so out of His/Her love for me, I to vow to stand by and assist the forever continuance of this Order.

This Order is the Order of Life and Death and I shall be reborn to it. My life is a caldron of eternal existence, hence my death only a bridge that spans the voids of reason. Be it for me, the world given by the God of Self and shall I seek only that what I need to survive. Through these words I declare to protect this world from all those who seek to destroy it and our children. At last, I have seen through the fiery eyes of the Dragon and He/She hath declare me a Soldier of Truth and so I shall lay down my life before the Order of Judgment. I hereby take my seat adjoined, One with this Holy Order. Through this Oath I submit to honor the Blood of my fellow Brothers and Sisters, by the same Blood that flows through my veins, "Blood of My Brothers' (Sisters') Blood!" Hail! Hail! Hail!

K.T.

The Oath
of
The Satanic Vampir

or

The Oath of Lust

**(This is the initiation oath
of
Satan's Vampir Army/Healers)**

I swear to honor The Cult of Blood, until I depart from its domain. I hail the power that gives the cult life. This power is the blood of our flesh, The Life-Force. This life essence has awakened me to the true Master found within myself, whom is Thy Eternal Lord, St. Vlad. So upon my knees I swear allegiance to the divine one, myself, and The Cult Of Blood. I hail you, Lord of The Satanic Vampir!

(This ritual is performed at midnight, The Witching Hour. The Head Priest or Priestess and initiate must be wearing their ceremonial garb. The initiate must be upon his or her knees, with their arms crossed in an Egyptian fashion, making The Sign of The Phoenix! The initiate must complete their oath by leaning forward in an act of faith, reaching toward the Priest/ess to perform The Sacred Kiss upon The Sacred Ring! The Priest/ess then places the necklace of the Serpent upon the neck of the initiate. This necklace bears The Symbol of Baphomet, The Inverted Pentagram. This symbol of death, truly symbolizes eternal rebirth, Eternal Life which the initiate reveals in the light of the new day, wearing the necklace bearing the symbol of true life, The Ankh. The Ankh symbolizes Eternal Resurrection, Eternal Life, Youth, and Beauty! By night the winged serpent Set rests and feeds upon its initiates and by day transforms into The Great Phoenix, flying across the Heavens bringing Renewed Life to all of Creation!)

Part VII Church Holy Days

The Great Saturnalia

"Saturday will be our day of joy and merriment!"

The Great Saturnalia, The Feast of Saturn has been chosen by The First Priest as our Sacred Festival. This is in correlation with the completion of his Holy Book, Satan's Divine Vampire Bible! This festival will last a week or two, beginning on the eve of the holiday! For on the 15, He had a vision of the hypocrisy of the world's religions. On the 16, of December 1999, The Holy Day of Pleasure began. This day of course will not end for a week or two. On this day, He had a revelation of the world's religions great demise! For in His Revelation was the completion of The Great Work! Each of our Brothers and Sisters will take The Sacred Sip, of The Sacred Wine, in remembrance and celebration of Our Triumph! There is the great and small, in all things! Therefore, we shall celebrate every Saturday, hereafter, remembering our Goddess/God, Ourselves, and Our Great Holiday, Our Holy Day of Pleasure! This will be our Night of The Sabbath! The lesser Sabbath will be a continuous event, hosted by our Brothers and Sisters! This event will only be open to members and initiates! Come join our celebration, Brothers and Sisters! For this is The Temple of Life!

Part VIII The Great House of Polygamy

Introduction

Polygamy is the advanced and beautiful lifestyle of having more than one bride or groom (polyandry). It is founded upon the belief and practice of polyamory which is the ability and willingness to love more than one other person, etc., at one time or the same time. It is also founded upon the desire and willingness to engage in promiscuous sex with as many partners as we choose and when we choose without discrimination or condemnation from inferior, idealistic, fanatical, and basically unnatural or non-carnal judeo-christian moral-values.

We publicly declare the right to defy judeo-christian dogma and civil laws, loving and wedding who we desire to and will to love and wed, when we wish to do so.

Our New Age Lifestyle is not exactly new it has been practiced by many ancient cultures, before the advent of judeo-christian monogamous fanaticism or fascism. There were many cultures that enjoyed monogamy, but they never condemned polygamy in the least.

Monogamy and Polygamy (polyandry) existed alongside each other happily, until the rise of such fanaticism/fascism. It is only those religions that don the judeo-christian banner and seek to institutionalize the dogmatic judeo-christian moral-value system that condemns polygamy.

Our goal is to rise to a higher more loving relationship, escaping greed, possession, jealousy, cheating, lies, fighting, and hating those you truly love. We seek to raise the status of maturity within the culture through moving beyond such inferior qualities, which we continue to pass on to our children. We intend to teach our children the superiorly divine beauty of sexuality, polyamory, and polygamy. Our future will not be filled with stagnate, oppressive beliefs out of the dark ages of human history. Our future will be filled with great beauty, joy, pleasure, and fulfillment beyond human imagination. We will send these useless, oppressive, false religions back to the darkest pits from which they've come. This is The Age of Fire! This is The Age of Humanity! This is The Age of The Great House of Polygamy!

Pre-Nuptials and Benefits

All family members that officially break ties with or divorce from the family, leave with what wealth they joined with, minus contributions to the family wealth or treasury. All members maintain separate treasuries at their will or according to the capability, based upon the type of economic system. All members enter into a Pre-Nuptial Agreement, which clarifies that all parties leave with what they joined with, minus contributions and personal choice expenses. The only ones that must receive benefits are children, and this comes out of the family treasury. These benefits don't have to be monetary.

The Individual

The individual is someone outside of all family houses that really has no title or power, within any House of Polygamy. They remain so until they wed into a family, wedding a Master or Mistress, or they apply for Master or Mistress Status. The individual and their children cannot receive benefits from the family treasury, only the Master or Mistresses personal treasury.

The Master or Mistress

Anyone who is a member of our church may apply for an Official Master or Mistress Title, which empowers you as the Master of your New House. The Master or Mistress is responsible for overseeing the House or Family Treasury and setting up most family regulations, such as contributions, work, benefits, etc. The Master may wed other Masters or Mistresses, combining their family treasury. If they divorce, family treasury is always divided according to what they wedded with, based upon Pre-Nuptial Agreement, minus losses, contributions, benefits, etc. A House of many Masters and Mistresses may appoint Lords or Ladies from among their family circle of Masters and Mistresses to oversee different functions and aspects of the family, and family business.

The Concubine

The Concubine is anyone without title, general family, or anyone who steps down from Master or Mistress, and Weds a Master or Mistress. The number of concubines or wives/grooms a Master or Mistress may have is unlimited. They have no major responsibilities overseeing family affairs and business.

General Family

General family includes children, teens, and anyone who remains in the family and does not apply for Master or Mistress Status.

The Royal Master or Royal Mistress

This is an In-House Status and they have no power over the affairs of the House they were born into, unless appointed by the overseers or if the overseers became completely inactive and or incapable of fulfilling their responsibilities on an average day to day basis.

Part IX Advanced Church Principles

The Principles of The Anti-christ Religion

1. **Anti-circumcision/Anti-baptism:** We are against circumcision! Circumcision is a sign of the jew and christian covenant to their god. This is a primitive practice which destroys the natural external beauty of the human body. We hold no covenant with the jew/christian god, only ourselves and creation. We are anti-baptism as well. Baptism represents the christian initiation ritual upon entering their church. This ritual is usually performed shortly after birth, to begin the child's inculcation and indoctrination as soon as possible. We abhor this practice and believe that any form of initiation must take place when a human is of a mature age of understanding, education, experience, and wisdom.

2. **Anti-monotheism:** We support polytheism, pantheism, and atheism. Having or holding more than one god or belief and respecting other deities/beliefs in mutual respect is superior to monotheism. Polytheism/Pantheism is the key to unity and everlasting harmony! –Pantheism should be known as the

Creationism and what is known as the christian creationism should be called zionist science. (Note: In the Hindu system the polytheist aspect is only another aspect of an underlying monotheist view. This is close to the system we represent and therefore our idea of Anti-monotheism is not a total opposition to all forms of monotheism. We want to make it clear we support the rights of those who choose different forms of religious beliefs, especially polytheist and pantheist!)

3. Anti-spirit worship: We support physical/material human body worship. We worship the beauty and pleasure of the human body! The human body is the highest and most important aspect of our existence and the ultimate object of our will and desires. We believe in worshipping the human body as an object of carnal reverence and sexual delight. The sacred carnal flesh is blessed with sacred sexuality! (Note: This is in no way meant to oppose the worship of natural spirits, energy forces, Shamanism, etc. which we find to be very spiritual and beautiful. This is about our opposition to the judeo-christian denial of the flesh and their complete focus upon the spirit.)

4. Anti-monogamy/Anti-marriage: We support polyamory, promiscuousness, polygamy, bigamy, polyandry, and misogamy. We support polygamy and stand for Anti-monogamy, and Anti-virgin purity. We support and teach Anti-marriage/misogamy or teach polygamy. We do not teach monogamy, but it is up to each individual to choose their lifestyle. (Note: This is about supporting the rights of those who wish to marry as many partners as they wish or the rights of those who hate marriage and do not wish to be married at all.)

5. Anti-heterosexuality: We support homosexuality and bisexuality. We are anti-heterosexual when it comes to the mainstream of society. Through teaching and spreading heterosexuality, homophobia and anti-gay beliefs are spread as well. Through that homophobic culture gays and bisexuals face extreme condemnation and discrimination. By teaching against total heterosexual lifestyles we eliminate the majority of homophobic and anti-gays beliefs and fears. This is not a stand against heterosexuality in general, meaning it will not arise as hatred toward heterosexuals because we teach and promote bisexuality. Heterosexuality becomes more than common place and typical among lifestyles that also embrace the same sex.

The total heterosexual will be rare and a minority, that will face little condemnation. We teach that we are born in a natural and beautiful bisexual or androgynous state. We therefore teach against a mainstream heterosexuality through a form of anti-heterosexuality, though it is up to each individual to choose their lifestyle. (Note: This is not meant to be a complete stand against heterosexuality, but we see a better society and civilization based upon bisexual foundations much like in many ancient cultures and civilizations.)

6. Anti-homogenization: We support religious, political, economic, and racial, etc., segregation (separation) on a higher level to ensure equality and respect the rights of those who believe in their type of environment. Mutual segregation (separation) is superior to homogenization, which is designed to limit, control, and empower only one specific belief system, or political/economic system. What this means is that those who wish to live in a homogenized state may do so and those that do not are free (should be free) to segregate (separate) into their own unified state or power.

Laws of Organizational Integrity

1. To defeat oppressive opponent religions you must secure power over them. Without power over them, they will forever advance upon you with beliefs, laws, guns, economically, etc., oppressing you with natural dominance. Through securing power over them the tables are turned.

2. Anti-religion does not secure power over oppressive opponent religions. This is because there will never be a world where the majority of people are Anti-religion or Anti-belief based. There will always be a dominant foundational core moral-value system.

3. Organized oppositional adversarial belief systems and religions secure power over opponent religions. True and Great Organizations are developed through allegiance and dedication to a Master Belief System and its ultimate goals. Great Organization alone is power over your opponents and a blockade to their progress.

4. The Constructive Unity and Conformity of your oppositional adversarial belief systems and religions secure power over opponent religions. Unity is synonymous with Conformity, when you stand before an opponent a thousand times your strength. The Individual Intelligence is Great but it is no match for the Gnashing of the jaws of the Multi-headed, Multi-intelligent Hydra. Alone you will be ripped to shredded pieces on the battlefield of Life and Existence.

5. Resistance to the organization must be eliminated within the inner ranks and those that pose a threat to the security of the order must be outcast. Inner turmoil and dispute creates violent

waves of destruction to the Social Skeleton of your Organization. The Social Skeleton must be at harmony with its branches. If voluntary members resist remove them from the center and place them near the outer reaches where they can do little harm stirring up a social calamity. Those that are a security risk must be watched and examined while kept far from your war rooms and secret meetings. Denigration may be employed toward the resistance factions as a military tactic keeping out the unwanted and keeping those who want to stay from thinking they can get away with the same behavior. Also, denigration may help to weaken the minds of the resistance factions.

6. Those dedicated and loyal to the organization must do some work to help advance the organization and build up its financial and substance based power structures. Organization Members can't just sit by idly and not take part in any of the work that the Organization is working toward. It is so important that the Members show their allegiance by taking part in one form or another, which will impact beneficially on the Order. This is True Loyalty, and anything less is Disloyalty and another sign of artificial conviction, and passive resistance.

Part X The New Church Sciences

The Laws of The New Social Sexual Psychology

1. Sex is a Need, not just a desire. Humans need to be sexually fulfilled, in order to escape sexual repression and attain maximum morale. The lack of sexual fulfillment, will lead to sexual repression, causing natural depression, anxiety, melancholy, collapse of self-esteem, collapse of self-confidence, etc. These natural personality traits or characters, can lead to more natural, yet external reactions that may harm the individual or others. These characters can manifest as suicidal tendencies, homicidal tendencies, and sexual assault or rape, etc.

2. Love is a Need, even if it is but a chemical emotion. The individual needs to be loved by another person or more, and also needs to love another person or more, to maintain an average mental state of health, which is based upon a degree of self-esteem, self-confidence, degree of motivation to accomplish some task or purpose, and a degree of social sexual libido, etc.

3. All Emotions, Feelings, Actions, and Reactions are Normal. There is no such concept of abnormality, or insanity, especially when dealing with the mind. There is not one thought, belief, or action that is abnormal. All attempts to abnormalize a feeling, action, or belief, is characterized by the influence of ones own moral beliefs and therefore it is a contamination of thought and diagnosis. This natural tendency to introduce ones own moral into the examination of another beings world, is part of our survival instincts, set on primeval domination. There is no way, to completely rid ourselves of such thought, because these

separate Laws of Animal Dominion can not be escaped, no matter how hard we try to ascend into our ideal spiritual nature. This in general means that, depression, suicide, war, rape, murder, pedophilia, etc., are all natural actions, based upon natural desires, emotions, and feelings. We must remember, we are not the judges of moral action, but the healers of natural symptoms. The old psychologists and psychiatrists became the guardian institutes sponsored by the governments and drug companies, to maintain and control those individuals that were mainly less criminal, and disrupted the flow of mainstream or the majority of society, with its dominant institutionalized moral-value system. Once again, this is a reflection of our Primeval Natures and the Laws of Animal Dominion. Since we too are forced into this position, we must endeavor to make sure that the dominant social sexual moral-value system is just, and free from fanaticism, since we have been placed in the position of judge and jury of the lesser gods and goddesses, The Super-Human Beings. (Note: This is not to be taken as approval of many of these activities but understood to be natural primeval human activities and natural states of mind!)

The Primeval Laws
of
Animal Dominion

There are four principle primeval laws of animal nature that will always exist. These laws concern all of animal dominion, but the study of our science is more directly concerned with all human social, cultural, economic, political, religious, and military societies or civilization, etc. No matter how civilized you claim to be or how religiously, spiritually, and morally fanatical you become, because of your ideal fantasies or programs, these laws shall rule over you.

Everyone who claims that violence and hatred are primitive actions and emotions is trying to or is enforcing their moral opinions, through these very same laws that in essence are of your nature. The question is not who is right or wrong. The question becomes, who is trying to dominate, using whatever belief as a tool or weapon to dominate? Most might never realize this, until it is pointed out to them. The belief itself

has power and used like a sword, harnesses more power, drawing in the like minded, which then reinforces their dominion, spreading it out further. We will gather together, based upon these laws of dominion, which dictates our universe. These laws transcend all human advancement, but can be used to benefit humanity.

According to our scientific laws, two great forces will always rise above the rest, and one will always dominate the other. We will eternally struggle to attain domination, escaping domination, or struggle to maintain our domination, fighting off being dominated.

First, you must understand what you believe and through this, whose side do you stand upon? There is no in-between, no neutrality, for in the end, there will only be two sides. Second, you must decide truly, whether you wish to be a leader or a non-leader.

The leaders will be educated members of an elite core that will carry the weight of responsibility, through all decision-making positions.

The non-leaders will engage in the act of receiving and fulfilling the precise and delicately calculated decisions passed down to them.

Third, you must invest in your beliefs, if you truly believe in them. This can be done through physical work, mental work, or economic and monetary support, etc.

Here are the four principle laws that dominate our lives:

1. Dominate or be dominated.
2. Strength in numbers.
3. New and better knowledge prevails over old and useless knowledge.
4. Order controls chaos.

Part XI Temple of Kama
or
Temple of Satanic Kali

Tantric Hindu Beliefs

Dharma, Ahimsa, Artha, Kama, and Yoga are the five main methods of spiritual enlightenment which all complement each other and represent proper ways of living. This would be according to the interpretations set forth here. I consider myself a Tantric Hindu. We use all the Hindu Scriptures, as well as others, and the Hindu Pantheon of Deities, to help us understand our lives and the universe. This gives us a sense of our purpose here and why and how we should live a spiritual life.

Ahimsa

Ahimsa is one of the main spiritual focuses of our Temple of Kama. Ahimsa means non-injury or nonviolence and a deep spiritual ideal of not harming other life forms. There are degrees of Ahimsa which we may try to respect when dealing with the practicality of situations. At all times we try to live a nonviolent existence which will help to eliminate karma and bring about a peaceful world in which to live and prosper spiritually. This happens by teaching Ahimsa along with our other ideals to help us achieve enlightenment through a spiritual health consciousness.

Dharma

Dharma is another one of our focuses. It represents divine truth, balance, and law. Here devotees are bound to the Dharma of our moral-value system, and other doctrines. Dharma can be said to be righteous living and we dedicate our lives to the Dharma. Dharma can also be associated with the idea of a judgment and the divine truth or life-force that fills the entire universe or Creation and is within every single one of us. We seek out the Dharma throughout our entire lives and it guides us to a state of liberation, freedom, or Moksha through our spiritual health consciousness.

Moksha

Moksha is liberation or freedom, much like nirvana or Samadhi. Moksha it is supposed to be liberation from the cycle of samsara or reincarnation and the end of suffering. This is only to be achieved through the Dharma or right living which includes the values set forth as the Dharma, Ahimsa, Kama, and Artha as set forth in our beliefs here. To practice Ahimsa, Kama, Dharma, and Artha properly as set forth here each involves sacrifice of the ego into the inner Self and Creation.

Karma

Karma is the idea of negative energies built up from negative actions and thoughts. These supposedly come back to us in out next lives. The idea is to live righteously and do good things for others and have good thoughts to eliminate Karma or negative Karma. Through this we escape the cycle of Samsara or reincarnation and achieve liberation Moksha. Karma is normally based upon the idea that each person has an individual soul and I believe that there is one great consciousness and so only one great soul. And each of us has to eliminate our Karma as one being to bring about a better world and to free those who seek freedom from the cycle of reincarnation which becomes a non-consecutive form of reincarnation in my system. The liberation is from the suffering but not life itself or Creation. And we have a choice to attain to living god-hood or eternal bliss. This can only be achieved through ego denial and unity dedicated to the spiritual health consciousness.

Non-Consecutive Reincarnation

Non-Consecutive Reincarnation is based upon the idea of a universal soul or life-force. We are but merely individual aspects of this great consciousness. We shall always exist and are reborn a thousand times before we ever die. This is like a great hydra with many heads and one dies. The creature does not die it only grows another head or many heads. Also, it's like a great ocean or lake. Out of the lake arises a life form and it lives its whole life and then returns to the lake and in an instant disburses into infinite particles that can never be traced and at all times new life forms are constantly emerging from the lake and returning.

Samsara

Samsara is the cycle of reincarnation which we go through until we eliminate Karmas and achieve Moksha. Though in my system we do not ever escape this cycle we only escape the suffering and live forever if we choose or we choose to embrace Nirvana or Moksha.

Spiritual Artha

Artha is known as prosperity and material wealth, though I see it as Spiritual and Material Wealth for all people in a state of super-equality brought about by the surrender of the ego to the inner-Self and Creation. Through this process all can attain to true prosperity together and live a very fulfilling life through the Temple and the Dharma of their Temple. Think of your Brothers and Sisters before your-Self and Spiritual Wealth before Material Wealth. Those that seek only material wealth for themselves are unspiritual and this goes against our spiritual health consciousness. It is seen that those who perpetuate a monetary system that create classes or those that created castes that then creates a monetary system do so only to maintain control and power through their own ego fulfillment and do not practice Spiritual Ahimsa and fall short of practicing the Dharma. They will have the greatest Karmas that hold all of humanity back as a whole being.

Sacred Kama

Kama is the idea of sensual and sexual fulfillment and spiritual enlightenment through Tantric Rituals. Kama means Sacred Love or Sacred Sex. Through union of the masculine and feminine aspects of Creation, or a God and Goddess all of Creation was brought into existence and expanded into the material universe. And so since humans are part of Creation they are divine deities as well which reflect the Creation and so through their ritual reenactment of Creation's Copulation they raise Kundulini and achieve divine spiritual consciousness or divine spiritual health consciousness and also the sensual fulfillments all creatures need to become and remain healthy. And the symbols of sexuality are divine symbols such as the phallus and vulva or the lingam and the yoni. And the human body is the most sacred temple of all. Through this consciousness raising we bring about universal spiritual health consciousness and so the sacredness of Tantrism is established. All supporters should practice Kama to achieve the Dharma, Ahimsa, proper Karma, Artha, and Moksha.

Yoga Enlightenment

Yoga is the path of physical and spiritual enlightenment and healthy living. There are said to be hundreds of forms of Yoga but 8 limbs or branches. Most are familiar with Hatha Yoga with its positions. Meditation Yoga and Tantric Yoga are a few that we teach in our Temple. The Priest or Priestess practices Dharma which teaches us to be spiritually and physically healthy and it is the job of the Priests and Priestesses to learn various healing arts and heal others and teach others. (Note: This is just a set of basic beliefs on our Tantric Hinduism. There are many deeper doctrines located in The Tantric Hindu Bible!)

Part XII Satanic Evolution The Fall of Laveyan Satanism

The Darkness of Laveyan Illusions

I have created my own New Denomination of Satanism, Vampir Satanism 999! First off, I'm anti-laveyian and I have a big problem with these so-called traditionalists. I just don't buy into that! I consider that, all part of the laveyian attempts to categorize and separate themselves from other denominations of Satanism so that they can try and claim a monopoly on what they are calling the only real Satanism. Most if not all of these other serious organized groups that allowed them-selves to be called and accept the term traditionalist, have only sprung up in the past hundred years or so and in my opinion they are clearly ALL contemporary Satanist Organizations!

There is a difference between laveyan Satanism and other denominations of Satanism, but I teach people not to buy into the whole, You're a Devil Worshiper and I'm a Real Satanist Bullshit!

That is the laveyan illusion, cast like a spell to blind you and misdirect you so that they may appease christians who say you worship the devil, you sacrifice un-baptized babies, etc., and more importantly so that they can claim the sole rights to Satanism! If they can mentally establish and convince you that they have the sole rights to Satanism, they can continue to guile their way into the thought and concept of declaring themselves to be the only true Satanists, which ultimately grants them

a monopolistic illusion that draws to the cos most of those members seeking to be the quote unquote "Real Satanist!" and of course all the profits with their Official Memberships!

My Beliefs can be considered in the light or I should say the DARKNESS of laveyan illusions, to be more of the Traditional BRAND! It would help you immensely to study my Satanic Vampir Bible, Satanic Vampir Creed, and also my Definitions of a Satanist 999!

Satanic Evolution

First of all, I'd like to remind everyone that the true purpose of this christian SHIT coming in here(Groups, Domains, Etc.) is to undermine our goals and slow our progress through antagonistic distractions. Our purpose in exposing christian motivations is apparent.

Our purpose in exposing these laveyans may not be so apparent to the younger and new follower of a forked Left-Hand Path! We are exposing their path as a Dead End on The Road of Satanic Evolution!

They have no higher goals and therefore have no real intention of ever attempting to actually overturn the judeo-christian moral-value system.

They believe that they are not victims, that they are not oppressed, and have no true rights! This is outrageous, self-denying and we won't stand for it!

The New Left-Hand Path has been cleared for the Youth and the New Initiate to walk upon and actually reach a True Set of Goals that we have set up to achieve for the good of the whole Satanic People! As for my saying that laveyans not being Real Satanists, this has been misconstrued and twisted by our pathetic local christian enemy! That is what they do, they twist, confuse, and disseminate false information as part of their infiltration and undermining tactics. This is why we must rid our clubs, groups, domains, etc., of them. It only leads me to believe that the mindless, brainwashed laveyan founders of these clubs, etc., are so trapped in the deceitful mercenary web lavey spun, that they can't think for themselves!

How do christians truly benefit you? The level of seriousness by the so-called Satanists in these clubs is zero. They have no concept of Religious Revolution or True Secular Change! If entertainment and basic socializing are your reasons for being here, then you're hopeless, lost, and worthless to any True Satanic Cause! What I said about laveyans is that they declare themselves the only Real Satanists, out of natural ego, personal reputation and popularity, and out of a need to create and stabilize a monopoly! What I said was laveyan Satanism is not even a Real Religion, it is just an Atheistic Philosophy. I never said that they were not Satanists. As for us, we are Real Religious Satanists!

Also, I never said I wasn't a hypocrite, though I have said many times, that I'm far less hypocritical for my beliefs and policies. I even state in my Satanic Bible that we are ALL hypocrites and if you say you're not, then you ARE a lying hypocrite! Does everyone here believe in hearsay or do you realize that most of what I say is calculated and what my enemies say is straight up bold-faced accusations and lies???

THE COS IS DOOMED

What's the matter, have the poor inferior and doomed laveyan Satanists finally realized that Anton was truly an insecure narcissist, cheap foolish con-man, a weak punk, and an evolutionary missing link or APE-LIKE BEAST reflecting upon the primitive and inferior philosophy he adopted??? Have you realized that the cos is facing inevitable destruction as its membership has completely ceased to grow??? Have you realized that My Policies and My Church of The Antichrist is FAR Superior to your own CRAP???

Well, get ready, you and your kind have had almost 40 years to prepare and prove your worth! What have you accomplished??? JACK SHIT! The cos is a big sickening failure in my book! It's time for the Superior anti-laveyan Satanists to rise above the inferior laveyan Satanists! It's time to TURN UP the heat! It's time to let the Cunning Jackal out of the bag! It's time to open the REAL gates of hell! It's time to teach you all what Superior Policies are all about! It's time to teach you a lesson known as a FORCE called the Church of The Antichrist!

The elite of the cos is nothing more than a fancy title for a bunch of low-life mercenaries, who are doomed to an anti-social undercurrent.

They are just another HERD of moronic atheists clinging to a pseudo-religion because they ARE too afraid to completely separate themselves from it. Even worse, they hypocritically cling to Christian doctrines, such as antinomianism! Hey barton why don't you beg for some more money to save the black house and fill your pockets some more? The cos is DOOMED! My curse is a curse of Will and MY WILL be upon you!

COS Antinomian
and
Objectivistic BULLSHIT

I've never said that it's impossible to have a monopoly on a religion. I said that no one or group should have a monopoly on it, because it defies our rights to believe in whatever we believe that particular religion to be. Therefore, we are standing against the bullshit that laveyans tell everyone, which is that they are the only REAL Satanists. They tell everyone that because that is one of their methods to building up and trying to maintain a monopoly on Satanism. Well, it's about time somebody exposed their LIES!

As for representing a true archetype of a Satanist, Satanism didn't become a real concept until christianity turned the Opposing Spirit of Satan into their Devil. Then only through the original Christian archetype the truest form of a Satanist can be determined! Laveyan Satanists are nothing but modern day Atheists, clinging to the heretical christian doctrine of antinomianism.

Laveyan Satanists pride themselves on their separation from the christian model, yet reveal another hypocrisy by clinging to their doctrines for support. A religious movement that is separating itself from christianity completely doesn't take on aspects of their doctrines and even the names of their enemies. This must be yet another publicity tactic! Doctrines like that must die with the church and their moral-value system. Any attempt to keep them alive is just a publicity stunt, to enrage the far right to run around screaming heresy! This is great for business, isn't it? If you truly wanted to defy their moral-laws, then you would keep focusing on their moral-value system in an attempt to ACTUALLY overturn it and not just talk about it!

Then laveyans mix that doctrine with the philosophy of objectivism.

Now, they run around declaring they defy their moral-laws, yet they don't have to fight against their moral-value system and actually work to overturn it because they are not victims of christianities oppression, they are not oppressed! This is another example of the blind leading the blind, or the enlightened, blinding their sheep! This is another example of their self-centeredness, since they may see no personal benefits in ACTUALLY fighting to and overturning the judeo-christian moral-value system which truly does oppress billions of people, through civil laws!

COS LIES

Now, we are talking about preaching, and converting, which all comes down to a recruitment policy. Every organization recruits to survive in one form or another and if they say they don't they are either lying to your face, extremely stupid, or both!

The cos declares publicly that they don't recruit! This is an outright LIE! After declaring publicly that they don't recruit, they hypocritically and covertly recruit their followers. Everything the cos and its members do, that publicly promotes the cos or its philosophy in one form or another, is a method of recruiting! This is not only a GREAT HYPOCRISY it is a far inferior and shabby method of recruitment!

All organizations that have come to any great level of achievement and expansion have done it through open and public recruitment! How do you think christianity got so powerful and far-reaching? They first, used an open and public recruitment policy! How does the military raise new troops? The military raises new troops through an open and public recruitment policy.

The Church Of The Antichrist has adopted this Superior and far less hypocritical Method of recruitment. Besides, I thought the cos was beyond playing on those ignorant inversions of christianity? Since, the christians try and convert us, we pathetic and half-witted laveyan Satanists have to go against Superior Methods of advancement, because we want quality over quantity. That is the most asinine thing I have ever heard of. The bulk of you laveyans should be ashamed of yourselves for such stupidity. Your leaders know what I'm talking about, since they are the ones perpetuating this fraud.

Laveyans and the cos have no higher goal which means they are all truly out for themselves. Therefore, it means that the cos is just an atheist's capitalistic dream business. In order for them to survive and pay their bills, they need quantity. Every jackass knows that quality always rises anyway. So, there is another LIE. The cos is truly after quantity, not quality! If they were truly intelligent, they'd stop selling you this garbage and adopt some real advanced and Superior Principles and Policies. Remember, that you all believe in absolute self-godhood so why wouldn't they be conning you for every cent you have? I'll tell you the truth though, they will collapse further and then reorganize and adopt very similar principles and policies as my own, because they are Superior Principles and Policies!

Laveyan Demise

It's about time another club or group owner has gotten up the guts to promote True Satanic Ideals! This is another victory for me since you are partially conforming to my Superior Policies! Your hypocrisy will undoubtedly shame this Great Satanic Deed if you allow christians and other Satanic enemies to violate this True Satanic Law!

Being the laveyan that you are, I suggest you restudy Pentagonal Revisionism! It is the christian infiltrator that you should be most worried about. My goal is ultimately to bring that to your attention and make you realize their true purpose here, which is to undermine your efforts and slow down your progress.

This is a small victory for Satanism on the grand scale and even if you don't get it, at least the Superiority of Segregation through the deletion of myself will be recognized and eventually spread and practiced, yet practiced in the true light of christian oppression through homogenization!

Christians and other enemies DON'T BELONG in our clubs, groups, domains, etc., which are miniature reflections of OUR world environments or habitats! To allow them access to your habitat just for publicity or entertainment is such a great hypocrisy in itself, especially when you delete those who are even greater and truer representatives of Satanism!

In my opinion laveyans reveal their true colors in this fashion, through showing the world that they are only out to personally capitalize on their satanic adornment or how childish and immature they really are enjoying the entertainment that these fanatical christians bring them without ever setting or seeking to achieve any REAL Satanic Goals!

Laveyanism is a dead and stagnate religion, with no true higher goals! This alone spells out your demise and the rise of Greater,

Truer, or more Realistic Satanism with True Satanic Goals for the whole of future Satanic Society!

COS FREES MANSON AND BIN LADEN

According to the Third-Point of the laveyan/cos's Pentagonal Revisionism, it sees men like Charles Manson and osama bin laden as Scapegoats and they should be given impunity or amnesty and set free! This scapegoating is seen as an extension of the judeo-christian cop out of blaming the devil for everything.

Therefore, men like Manson or bin laden become cast as a villain, a Devil! This reminds us of the laveyian satanic creed of Responsibility to the Responsible! In the case of the wtc and the pentagon, all the actual perpetrators perished with their victims, though the people demand that justice or retribution must be served! It is clear from this perspective that judeo-christian ideals influence the present justice system. Therefore, the Third-Point of laveyan/cos Pentagonal Revisionism stands against secularized religious beliefs, incorporated into law and order and calls for a return to Lex Talionis!

This means the feds., the government, would need a whole lot more evidence to go after bin laden and he would be treated as truly innocent until proven guilty of actually participating in the crime itself. Leave it up to the cos to free bin laden!

Lavey Was An Ape-Like Beast

The cos was founded on asinine and inferior principles, by a low-life mercenary who was a bigger evangelist than any right-wing fundamentalist! Lavey was an apelike beast walking on all fours to his grave, taking his mercenary and useless cos with him. The time has come for a Truly Evolved Satanic Religion and not some hypocritically inferior philosophy.

If lavey had brain one in his head, he knew that his adopted philosophy was doomed, only thinking about the notoriety and fame that he would attain in his lifetime. That is the philosophy he PREACHED from his pulpit, Self-Godhood and everything and everyone else was unimportant.

Now, lavey did one thing and one thing only, which I respect him for, because he was guided by the Satan of Divine Creation. He spread the word of SATAN to the eyes and ears of thousands, but his adopted philosophy is inferior and flawed! The time has come to burry the inferior and raise up the Superior through the Will of the True Master!

If you want to learn more about the inferior cos and the Superior beliefs of my Church of The Antichrist then talk to me. If you want to learn some potent Magickal Arts then talk to me. If you want to hear bullshit, listen to the cos evangelists/recruiters! We all have evangelists or recruiters but they'll just lie to you and say they don't do that. That is so hypocritical and such an inferior method of recruitment.

All great organizations rise up first out of an Open and Public Recruitment Policy. To learn more about cos lies and bullshit, COME TALK TO ME! Hail the Church of The Antichrist!

A New Satanic Leader

First of all flame-wars are good! They help to create the atmosphere and mentality needed to raise this much required war into a greater field or advance it to a higher scale externally, mainly socially and politically. This war is centered on our personal freedom, desires, and needs! It will be fought with or without your approval, because it is human/animal nature.
Through the study of our animal nature, we develop a science called, Animal Dominion! This science uncovers the authoritarian nature of the animal kingdom. Basically, this means when applied to humans that no matter what, one group of people, religion, or government will always dominate the other. In knowing this knowledge it is foolish to stand against Authoritarianism!
At this time christians still dominate the earth. What this all means is, it comes down to us and our children or them and their children. We will not be dominated and oppressed by christianity. This isn't about right and wrong, it's about our Will to Power, Our Personal Freedom, Desires, and Needs! Personally, I feel that I represent the most Realistic and Truest form of Satanism, The Superior Satanism 999!
These are admittedly really pathetic Satanic Clubs/Groups, but they ARE Satanic Clubs/Groups. Christians don't believe in magick, they believe in jesus, unless their hypocrites. Those that still believe in magick, cling to the old belief that it comes from their devil, their archenemy. These christians don't come into our Groups to debate and exchange theories on magick, sorcery, etc. They come in here to preach the dogmatic domination of their one-monotheistic god.
Well, their god doesn't exist to me and authoritarian christians certainly will never remain the dominate force on this planet

while I'm alive and my New Satanic Religion spreads to the True Left-Wing Masses!

Also, MANY OF THE SATANIC MEMBERS/SUPPORTERS ARE INTERESTED IN FIGHTING THEIR CHRISTIAN ENEMIES AND OPPRESSORS. They just need the right leaders, like me to show them the way! We don't need inferior mercenary laveyan scumbags teaching them that it's ok to be oppressed by your christian enemies and not to fight for rights they don't have. We don't need those who are not laveyan but like-minded enough to preach to them the same disloyal bullshit of total self-aggrandizement. We must build a Higher Satanic Unity, dedicated to the good of the Whole Satanic People, yet also fulfilling the Self. We will do this even if you stand in our way.

Through our Superiority, we will completely demolish all laveyan and like-minded outposts and run their businesses into the ground. You will join us or face your own economic extinction! If you wish to learn the Black Arts on a scale above these children, come and join our Church Of The Antichrist! The Black Arts are 90% Wisdom and 10% research! You don't need any books to learn the Black Arts, only if you enjoy reading and reading about other peoples success!

Laveyan Back Stabbers Part 1

You should check out my web site and read all my posts in all of the Satanic Clubs. Reading our site will give you a better idea of what Vampir Satanism 999 truly is about. I will say that the main differences that I see between the Left and right-hand Paths are very simple. The Left represents very sensible sensuous/carnal religions and beliefs, while the right represents totally non-sensible, non-sensuous, and anti-carnal religions and beliefs.

Look for The Definitions of a Satanist 999, The Satanic Vampir Creed, and especially My Satanic Vampir Bible called, Satan's Divine Vampir Bible, A New Moral-Value System! I will say that my belief system is political, economic, and religious! I feel that without any one of these social areas, we will have an incomplete religion! In my opinion, a true and great religion must encompass every area of interest that affects human civilization and the future of that civilization.

Laveyan Satanism stands against any future civilization, in a progressively spiritual state. We can be highly carnal and spiritual so don't be fooled by the terminology. They represent what I have called Puritan Individualism which is absolute self-deification, which represents pure mercenarism. This is the individual completely separated from society as an individual body. This system corresponds to the current capitalistic system which promotes total independence, which ultimately benefits the rich class at the expense of the poor.

Their atheistic system is not a real religion at all, just a philosophy. They are an anti-religion, because they stand against all forms of organized religion in general and as everyone knows, hypocritically incorporated as a church. This is obviously a business tactic. I could go on and on, because I have a whole list of things to reveal to those who want to find a better, Superior Left-Hand Path! My system does in no way stand against Self-Deification, but we recognize a Greater Deity of Creation, which we call Satan and it takes on anthropomorphic shape within us all as the Lesser deities of creation, but we are always one. Therefore, we are Satan!

Also, this is an Androgynous Deity or Creation, reflecting in our own human nature. Therefore, this is a Bi-Sexual Satan, Deity, Creation, or a Bi-Sexual God/Goddess! My system is not against the Self, it just puts the good of the whole higher than the individual. Therefore, my system incorporates a type of interdependence and has real goals that are realistic, for the future of higher human civilization.

Laveyan Back Stabbers Part 2

All of human civilization has arisen from our fantasy ideals and has been the greatest motivation, beyond self-interests that have pushed us on. Self-interests are fine, but when they become the higher goal of humanity, humanity becomes a cesspool of eternal stagnation and degeneration.

This form of capitalistic society actually breeds or cultivates and maintains a poor class to sustain the rich and middle classes. So, they have devised a system that will force billions to suffer eternally. Is this a sign of higher civilization? Do you want your children and their children's children to live in a form of manipulated and sustained poverty and suffering? The core of my system revolves around My Satanic Bible, which is a new moral-value system, designed to benefit the natural/spiritual birth-rights of all human beings. Some will argue that we have no rights, but I say that is based on the primitive nature of this divine world. In that sense, we have no rights, but we no longer live in that world completely.

The purpose of human society and civilization was to raise us from that jungle, to a higher state of spiritual existence. We just took or were forced down a wrong road, with nonsensical religions like judaism, islam, and especially christianity that stand against our carnal natures and self-fulfillment!

So, you see I'm not against Self-Fulfillment or Self-Interest, just emphasizing it over the good of the whole society and making it the absolute goal of humanity! Through Laveyan Satanism, everyone will tear each other apart, through greed, ambition, self-importance. These things are to be expected in society and are natural, you can't get rid of them, but if everyone followed that philosophy, society will truly rip itself apart.

One of the points of Superiority that I'd like to stress is that of the Loyalist over the mercenary. A group of mercenaries will destroy themselves, through that greed, ambition, self-importance, etc. While a group of Loyalists dedicated to a cause will fulfill what they set out and are determined to fulfill. A mercenary system is very weak and inferior, while a Loyalist system is strong and Superior. Therefore, a mercenary is symbolic of weakness and inferiority.

Many of those who contemplate this will be filled with fear, just at the thought of the Loyalist and their Loyalist Organization. The mercenary to me is the lowest piece of shit on this earth; which says exactly how I feel about Laveyan Satanists! If you think about it, you're already stabbed in the back, before you befriend them. If you have any serious questions, I'll try and answer them. Make sure you read over the documents I stated.

Laveyan Losers

To begin with, who the hell gave you the rights to the Satanic Mold? NO ONE HAS THE RIGHTS ON A SATANIC MONOPOLY! So, you can take your first rule and shove it up your asshole! Individuality is a given, but that is Individual Character, NOT total nonconformity. Total Nonconformity is the root of mercenarism and it is a big load of shit and the most inferiorly disgusting philosophy ever contrived.

The purpose of human society is to rise from our primeval state of existence into a higher more spiritually carnal existence. You are a mercenary piece of shit, just like lavey, yet he was inspired more deeply by the Divine Creation, which I call Satan! I know more about laveyan philosophy than you'll ever know, it is you who should read MORE closely. Lavey believed in everything I stand for, except my Constructive Conformity and NEW Satanic Moral-Value System, which is greatly needed for the future of Human and Satanic Civilization!

Laveyans have no goals, external deity, and stand against all forms of religion and higher society. You represent the lowest shit to ever crawl on the face of the earth and your philosophy is a degeneration of all Human Civilization into the foulest recesses of stagnation imaginable. This is why you are the ENEMY of Humankind and Satanic Advancement and Evolution!

Lavey talked about avoiding the Evolving Satanist, but SCREW HIM! He had the intellect of a clam! By the way, my personal life has been far more exciting than most of you jackasses can ever possibly dream about! KEEP DREAMING LOSERS!!! That is why the cos is on its KNEES, because all your kind can do is dream and live totally self-centered.

I have proven over and over the Superiority of my policies

and principles. Now, it's just a matter of time before the pathetic alien elite SURRENDERS to the True Satanic Allegiance! Hail Satan! Hail the Church of The Antichrist!

The False Laveyan Religion

THERE IS NO REAL SATANISTS! The ones who claim to be the real Satanists or the only true Satanists, ARE DEFINITELY NOT REAL OR THE ONLY TRUE SATANISTS! I noticed that it's mainly the laveyan Satanists and those who follow the same basic bullshit philosophy, who spread that nonsense about the true Satanist! Let's GET THIS STRAIGHT PEOPLE! No one person or organization has a monopoly on the rights to Satanism as a Religion!
So, everyone who runs around claiming that this is a true Satanist IS FULL OF SHIT! Also, laveyan Satanism isn't even a real religion, it's a philosophy! The reason I say this is because in order to be a true religion there are certain universal prerequisites that must be rationalized in order to be classified as a religion! 1. Your belief must include one or more external deities, outside the human-self! 2. Your belief must include a spiritual doctrine that will benefit humanity collectively, beyond individualistic needs and desires! 3. Your belief must include a higher or greater goal for humanity as a whole, beyond individualistic goals!
Laveyans are atheists and don't have a true exterior deity! Laveyans are mercenaries and could give a rat's ass about the Satanic People as a whole! Laveyans have only one goal that is their self-goal! So, in my opinion laveyans are not actual Satanists in a religious sense or do they follow a true religion. They are philosophical Satanists who stand by a philosophy that lavey adopted! That philosophy is eclectic of course combining many aspects of different philosophies, especially objectivism and a new age form of antinomianism. Then lavey renamed it Satanism!
I don't believe in most of the principles of objectivism or antinomianism. I find them to benefit the capitalist and only the

individual, when we need to be focused on the good of the whole society and the future of society! So, the truth is, there are no fundamental points to Satanism, no one has the right to claim a monopoly on these so-called rights, fundamentals and to claim they are the only truth! This is the same crap that christianity preaches, but laveyan hypocrites do the same thing. The pathetic cos has for years tried to push these concepts upon everyone until you swallowed them, which gives them the edge. I say no more, I'm ripping up the fake red welcoming carpet they tried so hard to roll out in an attempt to blind you from the truth.

So, whatever you personally believe Satanism to be is your truth and if they want to pretend that they represent and follow a real religion, that's their business. Though in the end, the Superior denomination of Satanism shall rise above all others!

CoS Stacks Idiot Upon Idiot

I guess it's true the cos is filled with idiots stacked upon idiots! Everyone knows that the cos and its self-centered followers could care less about anyone else's rights, that's why you drown yourselves in the bullshit called objectivism!

You believe that no one has any rights and that no one is oppressed!

So, it is quite obvious that the cos has FAILED the Satanic People as a Whole! You have no true intentions or goals of overturning the judeo-christian moral-value system and repealing specific laws in question.

You just don't give a shit and that's why every one of you are FUCKING SHIT and I will make sure the cos is pulverized!

You are all mercenary scum! It is my Church Of The Antichrist that TRULY has goals to completely overturn that system and repeal those laws in question, restoring our TRUE RIGHTS! As for whining, I am doing more work to attain these goals, than any other group; especially the idiot-plagued cos which is currently on its KNEES!

You say do something and then say why must I turn it into a cause? What kind of moronic statement is that? The CAUSE is the GREATEST WORK! Meaning while you sit here and allow hypocritical oppressive christians among your ranks and play fucking games of ridicule, we are gathering the TRUE COLLECTIVE needed to build political support to rise and secure what is Rightfully Ours!

It is CLEAR to me and everyone who isn't a moron that you have less of a life than me and it is my intelligence that will crush your foolishness once and for all!

If anyone here would like to help out and JOIN THE CAUSE, let me know! It won't be long before the cos is dissolved and The Eastern Satanic Alliance will be the Brightest Light in the Night and Early Morning Sky!

Through our Collectiveness and Superior Policies, we will restore our true rights! Any other way is truly futile and will exhaust our resources, skills, and Personal/Collective Life Energies! Hail Lvcifero!

Hail the Church of The Antichrist!

Spiritual Egalitarianism

Egalitarianism is a belief that all people are equal or a belief in social equality. This seems to me, to be more of a Spiritual Belief in the natural and spiritual birth-rights of all human beings.

We all deserve the same treatment, respect, social acceptance, and access to the same qualities of life. This stands true, provided that others are not treating us wrongly, disrespecting us, or blocking us through oppression from attaining the same qualities of life. Then we have a right, to disrespect them back, outcast them as they do us, and fight against their oppression, until we achieve the same qualities of life or the same opportunities to accessing those higher qualities.

Christianity and the rich-class do just that, they oppress us, disrespect us, and take away our opportunities to gaining access to these better and higher life qualities. Christianity does this through civil laws implemented through their majority and belief in their dogmatic moral-value system. The rich class and the middle class do this through controlling an economic system designed to maintain a majority lower/poor class. They also, do this through poorly thought out retirement plans, like social security and they suppress technology so that we are forced to depend upon the fossil fuel industries; which is a form of enslavement.

Now, I do believe that there are many people that are mentally and physically Superior to others, but this does not mean that they deserve better opportunities or better life qualities, just on that basis alone. I believe that there must be methods or a system that will offer everyone regardless of their personally Superior Abilities, a way to gain access to these Superior Qualities of Life! This means that regardless of how intelligent or how strong you are, meaning if you do brain work or you do physical labor, after 20 years, you both will have access to the same qualities of life. Anything else, is not only unfair, but is CORRUPT!

Laveyan Satanists, believe in Anti-egalitarianism! They like the current system that gives the intelligent the power to enslave the idiot. They like that type of Power, which is nature's Primeval World. They want society to remain in this primitive stagnate state, instead of rising to a Spiritual Apex, which will also be OUR CARNAL DELIVERANCE!

The current system promotes the lowest and most spiritually and socially backwards type of civilization which humankind has aspired to ascend from into higher realms of existence. This system is the most inferior, retched, lowlife, capitalistically mercenary shit ever invented!

The original form of capitalism was designed to help humankind, not oppress us and our children forever and ever, through Poverty Slavery!

Lavey's Heresy

I'm still waiting for an answer??? They have no answer, because they don't even know why, which means they haven't even got a clue as to the reasoning behind the beliefs they adopted. I think they just adopted them because lavey said this is the way to go.
Let me decipher this. They don't know what the fuck they believe in or its origins and the only reason they think they believe in it is cause they have their heads crammed so far up lavey's ass they've gone blind from believing this circus hustler's tall tales from the dark side! Let me clue in the rest of the laveyan beanie babies, etc. Antinomianism is a catholic/christian heretical doctrine, which means that you believe in faith over moral-law. This is a heresy. I'm telling you that the only reason lavey adopted a christian doctrine, is to make christians scream heresy, thus raising his and the cos's publicity level.
Lavey seems to twist this christian doctrine to his own use, by putting that faith in his self-god and defying christian moral-laws. Then they add the second hypocrisy to this formula of allowing christian moral laws to perpetuate, while they capitalize off their religion.
They do this by pumping Satan up, which attracts rebels and then deflates Satan into a pathetic little atheistic shih tzu (preferably pronounced shitzoo). Anyhow the second part is the bullshit called objectivism, through which they cling to an even bigger hypocrisy and lie.
They believe that they are not victims, nor do they believe that they are oppressed in anyway. This gives them the asinine idea that they don't need to be freed from oppression, they don't need their rights back, they don't need to overturn the judeo-christian moral-value system.

This is the most self-centered, self-denial of the reality that I have ever seen. Through this self-denial of their own oppression, the Ultimate Hypocrisy is born. They are using this objectivist nonsense as an excuse to turn the other cheek! I guess they enjoy cowering in the shadows and breaking christianities oppressive civil laws to fulfill their desires.

If you want to talk about Real Satanists, Real Satanists would FIGHT for their rights as a whole people. All laveyan Satanists, including lavey himself, were and are nothing more than lavey's psychic vampires, with their mercenary capitalistic beliefs. They will feed upon the weak, the poor, the sick. They are the true psychic vampires and they must be extinguished in the flames of Spiritual Progress, working toward our true Carnal Salvation! Laveyan Satanism is just a bump in the road, propelling us farther ahead and closer to our true Satanic Destiny!

Laveyan Stagnation and Christian Oppression

First off what they represent is complete self-godhood, meaning everyone else is shit compared to each one of them as an individual. If any group is a spin off the christian ideals of good versus evil, it's the laveyan group representing that evil. And they play it up for publicity.

That kind of mercenary philosophy, which is closely allied with capitalism in general, has only one way to go, that is no where, no advancement of any kind, no raising of society from its primeval state to a more spiritual plane. If anything, it represents a degeneration of society, back into primitive culture, remaining stagnate eternally, without progress. If men and women have no primeval rights, they shore as hell must have spiritual ones to secure. These laveyans don't believe that we have any rights whatsoever.

All of human civilization and society has arisen from our ideal fantasies, which is basically an attribution to our spiritual nature. It is the spiritual that sets up laws to defend our spiritual rights and secure us from primitive natures harm. Though, we also have certain spiritual rights, which are attributed to the carnal. Nonsensical religions such as christianity, judaism, and islam have denied us many of these carnal desires through setting up laws to enforce their dogma, leading us down a road toward a fanatical and nonsensical spiritual system that denies our human animal natures.

It is the goal of my church to not only raise us to a higher spiritual civilization, but to bring us also to our carnal salvation. Under a laveyan philosophy and christian domination, we would never secure our spiritual rights to our carnal sexual natures and our carnal technological ascension into a great humanly divine nature in this world or universe.

This is the question I have for you. Do you believe in your Higher Spiritual Rights, which of course harms no other Higher Being, unless harmed or injured by those others, and unless you need food to survive, or do you not believe that you have any rights to defend and secure at all?

These laveyans will never defend your spiritual rights, nor help you secure them. These judeo-christians will never return all of your rights to you and will continue to steal more of your rights, disrespecting and oppressing you further. It is my Church Of The Antichrist that boldly and gallantly declares to fight for, defend, and secure your spiritual rights eternally!

**Laveyan Lies
 and
 The CoS Demise**

Let's sum up what we know about lavey's bible and the cos. We won't even get into the personal bullshit about lavey's life. I'm sure that you've read all the facts.

1. He only wrote about a quarter of his bible.
2. He hypocritically added christian symbols.
3. Laveyanism is not a real religion, it is only a philosophy.
4. Laveyan philosophy combines antinomianism with objectivism.
5. To adopt a form of a heretical catholic doctrine such as antinomianism, is extremely hypocritical, especially for a belief system that is trying to free itself from christianity in general. Lavey and his publicity stunts, but wait they say they don't recruit? This is more hypocritical nonsense and bold-faced lies. Everything they do that promotes the cos is a form of recruitment. They stand against all organized religion, yet incorporate themselves and claim to be a real religion. More like a Real Business, than a Religion that serves and helps the people!
6. To adopt objectivism, is to say that you have no rights, are not a victim of christianities oppression, and actually means they don't believe that they are oppressed at all.
7. Since they don't believe they are oppressed they have no real goal of actually overturning the judeo-christian moral-value system. If they say they do, it's all talk.
8. If laveyan philosophy prevails, then the judeo-christian moral-value system will never be overturned, and the laws that

take away our true birthrights will always remain intact. This also means that judeo-christianity will always dominate all legislation and of course, The Satanist!

9. If the laveyan philosophy has no real higher goals for the Satanic People as a Whole, then laveyanism is truly a stagnate and dead religion going nowhere. They will always remain a minority in society, under christian authority. This is their alien elite, a group of minority atheists clinging to a mercenary philosophy, like a bunch of rats hiding in the dark corners of the world, biting and tearing each others heads
off to survive! Everyone knows that a group of Loyalists is far more Powerful and Superior to a group of mercenaries.

10. How can a bunch of atheists grouped together for support be considered a real religion? How can they ever believe that they will become a majority group? They don't, thus the alien elite. Therefore, the laveyan philosophy which stands against all organized religion is an Anti-Religion, which is more idealistic than the ideal religions! This is because there will never be a world with a majority of atheists and to seek a world that is such is far more idealistic than christianity!

11. The only true way to overturn the judeo-christian moral-value system is through a Real Religion, which must become the Majority! This is the Birth of a Real Religion, Satanism 999! As I've said before, Satanism must become Satanism 999!

Part XIII The Nine Satanic Statements

The Nine Satanic Statements

1. There is no true Satanism, only your Satanism. One dogma begets another. A single person or group can never claim a monopoly on any religion. Here you will find Satanism 999.

2. The Satanist seeks out those like themselves to form a constructive and interdependent union which is the foundation of positive and constructive conformity. Those who seek pure independence should do so and find themselves outside of our group and enemies of the greater cause. Alliances with other groups are encouraged as long as the beliefs and goals are not completely oppositional.

3. The Satanist believes in a deity of creation, a deity within themselves, or both. What has religion become when you have completely removed the spirituality, mysticism, and sacred aspects from its foundation? Religion collapses into an ugly creature that has no breath of life and can only simply be called a philosophy. This if it can be called religion, is a dead religion. Without a deity of some sort to centralize your focus and creative wills, the need for that religion becomes futile and all worship degenerates into self gain and defilement of the sacred. The beauty of religion is in its grand architecture built upon a foundation of faith in some unknowable force rising up into its pillars of ecstasy. Blind devotion is only blind devotion when you are not allowed to ask why and question your faith or allegiance in some unknown entity or force.

4. The Satanist has individual personality and character but does not seek total independence from the group unless they have chosen to be their own group. As their own group they become an enemy of the greater group and may not be

respected or allied with depending upon how oppositional they have become.

5. The Satanist recruits as many other Satanists as possible. Strength in numbers always prevails and quality always rises anyway. Those that oppose open recruitment reveal their hypocrisy and are of their own group and an enemy to the greater cause.

6. The Satanist accepts the anti-christian or Satanic Moral-Value System in order to create balance where chaos has lurked in a vacuum of emptiness created by the elimination of the judeo-christian value-system. Where there is chaos order must always rise. Anarchy is an illusion that never lasts long.

7. The Satanist must always be loyal to their personal Temple or Church. If they are not loyal to one outside they will be loyal to one within. Disloyalty of any kind is forbidden and represents the work of the enemy. First a Satanist must find loyalty within, and then can choose a Temple outside them-self. All are born in the light of the disloyal minion and find the light of the loyal god/goddess of creation that we call Satan within or without.

8. The Satanist is the Super-Man and Super-Woman rising in absolute dominance against their opposition as an allied Super-Race within one body or structure known as The Alpha Force. Those that separate from The Alpha Force will feel its current, its power bearing down on them as individuals they will be no match for The Alpha Force. This is the path of superior attainment within the Super-Collective reflected in the Super-Self as godhood and goddess-hood.

9. The Satanist seeks out the most advanced knowledge, skills, arts, beliefs, sciences, and spirituality to become a complete universal being. The Satanist uses this knowledge to advance the whole Super-Collective. Old and useless knowledge is archived and burned away spiritually as the new is ritually accepted and used to advance our cause to attain mastery of ourselves and our universe. As ants in a giant's world, the giants step upon the ants until the ants collectively overpower the giants by covering his whole body. Then the giant will recognize our power, accept our Alpha Force, giving us our rights, free reign, etc., and either work with us or be destroyed.

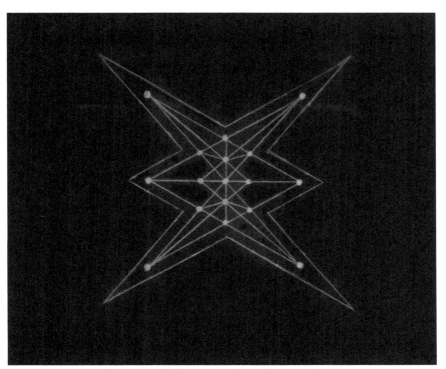

Star of Satanic Creation

www.ingramcontent.com/pod-product-compliance
Lightning Source LLC
LaVergne TN
LVHW011657020325
804901LV00011B/981